AF540019

Once Upon the Queens

Once Upon the Queens

GENDER UPTURNED FOLKTALES FROM BENGAL

SATABDI DAS

Translated from the Bengali by Nadia Imam
Illustrated by Paramita Brahmachari

An Imprint of *The Antonym Collections*

An Imprint of The Antonym Collections

theantonymmag.com

151, D.H Road, Kolkata 700 104, India

Published by Jilipi, The Antonym Collections, 2024

ISBN 978-81-976848-9-0

Book layout Designed by Tanmoy Dasgupta

Printed and bound in India by

Pixcel India
info.pixcel@gmail.com

Dedication

To the extraordinary compiler of stories
Dakshinaranjan Mitra Majumdar

A Few Words For the Grown Ups

What is a fairy tale? It is an optimistic, delightful story—a dream of respite that elders weave for their little ones to protect them while also preparing them secretly for the world of worries and obstacles. They are full of strange events, offering the child the joy of touching new horizons and feeling the excitement of the expedition, the hero undertakes. But in the end, a status quo is bound to be maintained, where the child feels secure, thinking that the dangers are over, and there is no room for regrets or complaints. These stories start from 'once upon a time', then overcome the 'evil', and finally return to an equilibrium of 'happily ever after'. The 'good' and the 'bad' are outlined or demarcated. For example, *Rajamoshai*, the king, is good; *Rakshasa*, the demon, is terrible; Queen Suyorani is bad; Queen Duyorani is good; and so on.

If you think about it, it is easy to understand that the concept of 'good' and 'evil', as described in fairy tales, is socially constructed. The intention is for children to learn to perceive what is considered "good" in social terms as "good"—this is the essence of the fairy tale's construction. Fairy tales seldom explore the many grays between blacks and whites and the extremes of good and evil. This may be reasonable, as children's minds are used to quickly perceiving binaries. During language learning, they memorize "opposite words." It takes them quite a while to realize this binary is shattered if they wish to explore it. Sometimes, even adults spend their entire lives in a binary mindset. But this "dual" fairy tale world for children is also created by adults! Adults' attraction to binaries is, therefore, undeniable.

Again, what is this relief of reaching the 'status quo'? The status quo exists for a reason; it represents a social stability that resists change and is expected to continue forever, perhaps to the discomfort of some marginalized people.

All the fairy tales end with the sentence, "Then the king ruled the country with prosperity and happiness." We hardly get to know how happy the subjects are. Or, when it is said, "Then they began to live happily ever after," there is an unwritten taboo against breaking up the family structure, even if its members are subjected to insult or torture.

The sense of right and wrong has a traditional name: values or morality. Fairy tales offer children lessons on morals or values in the guise of stories. However, if the 'values' they are taught do not change over time, they may not be of value anymore; they may lead to narrow-mindedness. They can also be called 'evil'. In extreme cases, they can even become as harmful as a crime.

Let's give an example. We have read in ancient texts that King Harishchandra sold his wife and son to prove his commitment to the truth. Many tears have been shed over the tale in the past. People in that era were convinced that Harishchandra had nothing else to do by weighing the story on the scale of their values. "Did the poor man's chest not burst?" They must have asked. "But the responsibility of protecting the truth was greater than the lives of one's wife and son." No one wondered whether Harishchandra had the right to sell his wife and son as assets.

Let us consider what would happen if the same events occurred in this century. Is there not a man in India now obligated to sell his son, his wife, or both? Sure, there is. In their view, they may also have their compulsions. But if such an event happens now, society will say in unison, "No matter how difficult it is, how can he sell his wife and son? So cruel!" Those more aware will ask, "Where did the man get the right to do this? Is he the owner of his wife and son?" Finally, those familiar with the country's current laws will say, "This act is 'illegal'. Let's file a case against the man."

What does it mean? To put it bluntly, values have changed a lot. That is, values are not constant. They vary from time to time, sometimes even from place to place. Our adverse reaction to today's Harishchandra (if there is one) is not 'value-free' but newly evaluated.

In the same way, what if the standard of 'good' and 'bad' is the same for the fairy tales that today's children read? We tell girls stories about the sleeping princess, who does nothing but sleep lazily and waits to be rescued. At the same time, we say to young girls, "Girls can do anything they want!" Isn't that a contradiction? Children see that the girls in fairy tales don't actually do anything. Being passive, docile, and submissive is the guiding principle of their lives. If a girl mistakenly becomes proactive, she is labeled the 'bad girl' of the story. Likewise, the young boy learns that his only job is to gallop on horseback. He must accomplish all manner of impossible tasks. He doesn't have the luxury of rest or respite. He must be a 'hero'—otherwise, he will have neither a kingdom nor a princess to his name.

So, when it comes to telling fairy tales to children today, we should reconsider the criteria of good and evil. Do they imbibe the changed (and forever changing) understanding of societal norms, relations, and values?

On the other hand, if there is even a glimpse of uncertainty about returning to the previously established 'status quo', the child will not enjoy listening to or reading fairy tales. So, we have to keep the status quo, but its content should be revised instead.

Maintaining this consistency is tricky because it is paradoxical: a 'status quo' that has 'changed'! That change should be brought in such a manner that it comes smoothly and rapidly. It is as if good sense has dawned on us collectively, and we as a society have eagerly embraced the new. This is unrealistic. But fairy tales have always presented reality clothed in the robes of fiction. Therein lies its craft.

Here comes another question. Do today's children read or listen to fairy tales? Many will opine that whether or not they read them in English, they don't read Bengali fairy tales! They have many other engaging ways to spend their leisure time. Moreover, the black-and-white printed letters have long lost the battle to the all-pervasive audio-visual medium! Fairy tales are told to them through motion pictures, called 'animated films', that offer them minute details and allow them to enter a realm of wish fulfillment. Or a picture book called a 'graphic novel'. The genre of appeal and medium of comfort have changed, and those new horizons have long taken care of Disney and Studio Ghibli.

But more is required than just changing the medium and style! As we said before, values change, and society changes. So, the content also has to change to keep pace. Old stories must be told again; they must transform. For example, the Disney Princess has changed a lot. They are no longer passive, helpless damsels in distress. They take part in all the adventures. Organizations like Disney run according to the dictates of the market. The fact that they are implementing these changes means an enormous societal recognition of this change.

The capitalist entertainment industry retells and recreates older stories for the larger global village market; it is bound to exclude the native, the local, the colonial, and the rural. Children, therefore, are introduced to the universally accepted newer set of ethics, but the native elements that the local culture transpires remain beyond their grasp. For instance, Cinderella is universal, but she is also Eurocentric. She dances and balls and wears gowns. And even if her story is retold, she may go to a night school instead of hankering after Prince Charming and his grand balls. She may become a wise woman one day, yet she will remain a white lady to an Indian child. What if we change the geographical location of Cinderella along with the then value system? That is doable but is quite an uphill task.

But there remains one more thing to be done. Or one more urgent task should be done. There is no shortage of fairy tales in our folk tradition—there never was! They carry in their very bodies the watermark of the native culture. They tell the stories of a pre-colonized, pre-globalized world that may seem a far-off land to today's child. Who will hand over to the child the remains of that world? Can't we tell them, then, our own lost stories in a new way?

This is the reason for choosing Dakshinaranjan Mitra Majumder. He was an exceptional collector and compiler of rural folktales. In the early twentieth century, as a newly awakened nationalist with an anti-colonial outlook and a deep affection for the folk culture and the stories of rural Bengal, Dakshinaranjan traveled to villages in Dhaka-Mymensingh and collected many stories. He put them into writing by first recording them on a wax record with a phonograph and then listening to them repeatedly. He saw that with the change of narrator, the narrative also gets altered bit by bit. Again, when Dakshinaranjan, the compiler, recorded the stories, he carefully changed them if necessary. With Rabindranath's help, this collection was published in 1907 under the name *Thakumar Jhuli*. This is how the oral tradition and the written literature merge. Rabindranath writes, "What else is there in our country as *Swadeshi* (Nationalist) as *Thakumar Jhuli*?" At that time, the elite intellectuals of Bengal were trying hard to return to the Swadeshi to revolt against subjugation; the *Lokayat* (folk) tradition was considered the way out. In *Thakumar Jhuli*, Rabindranath finds "our eternal social nature."

There is some difficulty here. Tagore appears to be more preoccupied with the decline of his people from the heights of their native culture into the depths of colonial foreignness rather than focusing on an evaluation of folk culture itself. Simply put, Lokayat culture is the 'object of study', not a 'subject with agency'. Dakshinaranjan or Rabindranath did not read the stories as someone from the Lokayat culture would have read it. The purpose and nature of their adoption are different. Does that mean that reading a text may depend on the social location of the reader, too?

If that's the case, why wouldn't the reading of someone like me, belonging to a different gender and time, be different?

Can we call the 'text' eternal? Change is the only 'eternal'.

As mentioned earlier, Dakshinaranjan perceived how stories change a bit every time the narrator changes. Therefore, when a narrator, who is none but me in this case, chooses to rewrite them a century later, the stories have to change.

The stories in the book *Thakumar Jhuli* are divided into three sections. I have chosen a few stories from each section to retell.

The first part is titled 'Dudher Sagar'. From this section, 'The Sleeping Kingdom', 'Kalawati', 'Kanchanmala', 'Kakanmala', and 'Seven Brothers Champa' have been selected for retelling.

The next part is called 'Ruptarasi', and from here, 'Prince Red Lotus, Prince Blue Lotus', and 'Golden Stick, Silver Stick' have been retold. They are the fifth and sixth stories of this book, respectively.

The last part is called 'Chyang Bang', and the stories selected from this section for rewriting are 'Fox Priest', 'Shukhu Dukhu', and 'The One And A Half Finger'. These are this book's seventh, eighth, and ninth stories.

Another collection by Dakshinaranjan was published in 1909, titled *Bongopanyas: Thakurdadaar Jhuli*. The stories of *Thakurdadaar Jhuli* are not just for children; they also serve as the balm for the young man's yearning for love or as a comforting companion for the older man's leisure. So, the compiler added the word "Bongoponyas" to its title. Here, we find more explicit socio-ethical recitations aimed primarily at women's moral education and how they would become dutiful wives. Compiler Dakshinaranjan told us that these stories were told on various family occasions. The girl who had heard the stories of *Thakumar Jhuli* as a child has now grown up. Now, she must be reminded of her duties, not politely but sternly.

Since our book is mainly for children, only one story from *Thakurdadaar Jhuli* has been selected as a representative story. 'Malanchamala' became the tenth story of my book.

When Dakshinaranjan gave written form to the oral tradition, although he wrote it mainly in prose, he created a poetic ambiance. Not only were there rhyming verses at the book's beginning and end, but each story is also infused with rhyming couplets here and there. This has created an illusion of the oral storytelling tradition. To keep the mood intact, the present recreator felt that newer rhyming verses should be included and tried her hand at poetry, which is an audacity in its own right.

I have named the first section 'Something to think about!' Here, I offer a thought. I want the child's imagination to fly to infinity as the thread is released. If parents could please help them, I would be greatly obliged. The second part is called 'The story of the story'. Its purpose is as simple as the name. The main story or old story is told very briefly. Parents and children will easily understand where, why, and what has been changed by the present author.

I warmly thank Antonym Collections for allowing me to embark on such a project. When the project's ideation was narrated, I thought, "Yes, this is what I wished to do for a long time." It is an author's pleasure to be bestowed with the opportunity of such creative experimentation. Thanks to Paramita Brahmachari for beautifully illustrating the book.

Each deconstruction is a new construction as well. So is this text. This text can be called the dream creation of a fairy tale. Or a fairy tale of how to create a dream.

Thank you

Satabdi Das
30/6/2024

And, For the Young Ones

The new dawn smiles there in the sky so blue,
A smile flashed on Khuku-Khoka's lips, too.
A sudden gust of wind in the Tepantar,
Changed dreams for Khoka, and Khuku wants more.
By the Khirnadi, a parrot of pure gold
When Father returns, they run to him to hold.
Grandma, Grandpa, their treasure trove of yarns,
Mother brought a worn-out pen, full of charms.
It writes new stories, a new land of dreams,
Let new tune and rhythm that make all laugh and beam.

The Sleeping Kingdom

1

Once upon a time, a queen and her king ruled a vast kingdom. Soon, they were blessed with a little girl in their arms.

As the days turned into years, the kingdom came aglow with the princess's virtues. Oh, such brilliance! How very kind and heartwarmingly radiant she was! People could hardly stop praising her.

Then, one day, our dear princess, now a wonderful young lady, looked up and around and felt "Gah! Terrible!" Dancing, singing, playing, studying, hunting—she had had enough. Too many comforts, had her days chock-full . . . what lay beyond and after and over there? She must see the outside world. The world outside! Wouldn't a trip be just it? Wouldn't it be grand if she went on a trip?

The faces of her subjects turned glum, and lines of worry sprang up on the queen's forehead. The agitated king forgot even to eat and sleep!

"Alright, let her go," the queen ultimately said.

"What are you saying? She is as precious to us as the treasure collected by seven kings!" said the king.

"Hush, you!" said the queen. "My father also spewed such nonsense and stopped me from exploring the world. Let her go!"

If sun and rain, she doesn't know,
How in the shade will she grow?
Her people's lives, her people's fears,
Their dreams, joys, hopes, and tears.

How upon the mountaintops,
Rainbow colors flip and flop?
Let the world be her school.
Only then will she be fit to rule!"

The people came bearing gifts for the departing princess. "At least, let guards and attendants follow her," pleaded the king.

"Only if she wants," the queen replied. "Otherwise, she can leave everything behind."

The princess took neither guards nor gems, neither attendants nor accessories of any kind. She packed only the beautiful blue dress she had been given on her eighteenth birthday and a few essentials for the journey. She secured her sword in its sheath, her brushes and paints to capture all the sights she would see on her way, and a few rolls of parchment to write down all the lessons she would learn. The princess then left for her grand tour of the world alone.

2

She walked for miles, crossing the mountains, rivers, and oceans. Sometimes, she painted the sights that left her mesmerized; sometimes, she simply stored them in her mind. Oh, what conversations she had with people! There were so many different kinds of them—such a variety of clothes, languages, and lives! Then, she arrived at the edge of a forest.

A great silence prevailed all around—not a bird chirped, not a branch swayed, not a murmur in the bushes, not even a roar or whistling in the winds. The land seemed frozen in silence. The princess stepped inside.

Hidden in the forest was an entire kingdom, with a gate as wide as a mountain range. Its highest spire rose up to pinch the clouds. But there were neither trumpets nor guards anywhere. The princess went in, and no one stopped or questioned her.

She heard no sound on her way. The pathways gleamed and sparkled with a milky white glow. Not people, but their statues stood lined up. All the royal carriages and carts were frozen. The leaves did not move, and birds did not fly.

The princess was astonished. Her hands, feet, and entire being itched to unleash that sword and vanquish this sleepy haze with a single strike! Oh, how she wished for the slumbering kingdom to move, dance, chatter, and chirp!

But wishes seldom come true instantly. After all, can every obstacle be overcome with a sword? How could she know who to kill and who to save without knowing the root of the problem?

Thus, the princess wandered about, curiously observing all she saw. Then, all of a sudden, the grand palace of the kingdom was right in front of her. And this time, the elephants and horses, guards and sentries, even an entire army stood there frozen in its vast courtyard.

"Can you hear me?" The princess called.

No one replied.

No one even looked at her.

Surprised, the princess went closer. Row after row of people and animals had turned to stone! Their eyes did not blink. Even the hair on their bodies did not move, let alone the hair on their heads!

The princess tiptoed into the palace full of rooms. She came across one massive armory with swords, shields, bows, and arrows in the thousands! But what if thieves came to loot it? Who would stand guard now that everyone here were stone figurines? What if even the thieves and bandits had been turned to stone in this cursed land? The princess slowly went ahead, holding the sword.

She entered the royal court. The golden lamp's flame was still burning, and the walls were encrusted with gems and jewels. But the king and the queen on their thrones had turned to stone. Ministers, sentries, friends, and courtiers all stood motionless.

The crown was falling off the king's head, leaning toward the west. The fan was slipping from the hands of the *pankhawali*—the fan-maid. What could the princess do? She exited quietly.

And entered a chamber full of a hundred lamps burning brightly—oh no, there were no lamps but jewels and gems—diamonds from the deepest mines and pearls from the hearts of the oceans. This, then, must be the treasury. But the princess felt no greed. She simply went ahead without touching a single treasure.

The fragrance of a thousand flowers wafted in through the princess's nose even before she entered the last room. Where did such a beautiful fragrance come from? Where was the garden? The princess found no garden; instead, in the middle of the room was a pretty little pond full of a mesmerizing bloom of lotuses—so many that they had covered the water. The scent of the lotuses filled the air. The princess stepped closer. Who was that amidst all the flowers?

A bed made of gold rested in the pond among the flowers. It had a diamond stalk, upon which a flower garland swung. Beneath it, was a prince laid whose beauty shone over all the jewels of gold, silver, diamonds, and pearls in the land. His hands and feet could not be seen; they were hidden beneath the flowers. Only his face, like a waning moon peeking out from between wisps of clouds, could be seen amidst the lotuses. The princess had never seen such a young man before. She had never taken such a liking to someone. She leaned against the diamond stalk with its pearl frill and looked at him with amazement.

3

Who knows how long it took for her spell to break? She remembered that her parents had taught her that she shouldn't stare at someone or touch them without their permission. The princess felt embarrassed. But how could she introduce herself to this young man, express her liking for him, or seek his permission? His sleep was so deep that she did not know when he would wake.

Suddenly, she spotted a golden stick near the prince's head. Slowly, the princess picked it up and held it; she saw a silver stick kept there, too. She started examining both closely, prodding them, turning them around in her hands.

When the princess was done, she went to keep both sticks back. She was mistakenly going to place the silver stick where the golden one had previously lain and the golden stick in the place of the silver one. *What would it be like if the two sticks were exchanged?* the princess thought.

The sea of lotuses shook the moment the sticks were swapped places. The golden bed stirred. Golden petals fell away, revealing the prince's hands and feet. There was life in his body again! The prince stretched and rubbed his eyes, jolting wide awake when he opened them. He sat up in his bed.

Immediately, a breeze started blowing. Birds began to call and chirp. Elephants began to trumpet, and horses neighed. A doorman called, "Hark!"

The royal court had woken up too—the king and the queen, ministers and sentries, courtiers and friends—all had arisen. All those who lived in the kingdom awoke from their thousand-year sleep. The soldiers and lords straightened up in attention with their bows, arrows, shields, and swords.

Amazed, they wondered, "Who was this? Some angel or magician?"

On the other side of the palace, the prince and princess gazed at each other, their glances flowing with love. “Why did everyone in your kingdom fall asleep?” the princess asked.

“Where do I begin?” said the prince. “My family has ruled this kingdom for fourteen generations. Everything was done just as the first king decreed it. There was no change in the rules. No one kept up with the times.

“The king ruled, and the queen stayed veiled in her quarters. The people bowed down to the king, and soldiers fought like wooden puppets at his command. The ministers did not give any new ideas.

“I used to study the rules set down by my great-great-great-great-great-grandfather as texts in school. I wielded my sword to the right if they asked me to. Left, if they said so.”

“What a nuisance! Wouldn’t this bother you? Wouldn’t you feel bored?” the princess asked.

“Oh, but we were all wrapped up in gold. We didn’t feel the pain. We were all intoxicated by the fragrance of musk,” the prince replied.

“Then?” the princess asked.

“Then came a hoard of demons. They possessed magical powers. We were ready to battle, but they said, ‘Oh, dear me! You lot are sleeping on your feet! Dead while you’re alive! How can you poor things fight a war? Why don’t you truly fall asleep instead?’ ”

“What!” the princess exclaimed.

“They snapped their fingers next,” the prince said. “And the whole kingdom fell into a never-waking sleep.”

He took a deep breath. “There was an old grandma demon amongst them. She had a little compassion in her. She said, “Thy Kingdom Will Once Again Wake, When She Cometh, for who, All Rules Breaks.’ She must have been talking about you!”

4

The royal court was in a state of chaos. As soon as she woke up, the queen opened her veil and said, “I will also give my opinion on affairs of state; damn your kingdom otherwise!”

“My hands ache to swing this fan,” said the pankhawali. “I want a day off every week and a salary increase of thirteen coins!”

The Prime Minister gravely set off to hunt for newspapers—how long had it been since he kept news of the outside world?

The sepoys said they were proud to sacrifice their lives for the safety of the land. But they needed proper remuneration and compensation in return.

Meanwhile, the king began to sing, "We are all kings in this kingly land!"

Amidst the commotion, everyone set off to find the magician who had blown away the cloud of sleep from over the land. Searching here and there, they ultimately came to the prince's lotus room, where they found him engrossed in conversation with a young woman. She was the magical one, the prince informed all. Trumpets, horns, and the beat of drums sounded around the kingdom.

"Which heaven have you descended from, o goddess, that you could break our death-like sleep?" the queen asked.

"Who are you, young lady?" The people wanted to know. "You soothed our souls. And your talents are unparalleled! You brought springtime to our golden kingdom that was buried under snow."

"I fiddled around with the golden and silver sticks; my playfulness was the real magic. I'm the flesh of my mother's flesh and the bone of my father's bone. How does it matter where they hail from or who they are?"

"Nothing matters," said the prince. "Your courage makes you a queen of the world and heart."

The princess then turned to the king and queen, saying, "If the prince agrees, I would like him as my companion and playmate for the rest of our lives."

If this were in old times, the king's forehead would be creased with worry, and the ministers would fly into a rage. Who was this girl? What was her lineage? How dare she say something like that? Soldiers would come rushing at her.

Now, they all happily chorused, "So be it!"

Everything has changed. This was now a new land.

Flowers were showered, sandalwood water sprinkled, and flowers happily grew on trees. Tongues could not stop wagging in excitement. The beat of a thousand drums echoed all around. Boys and girls gathered to make spice pastes and cut vegetables for the grand feast.

Auspicious vases are welcome at every door,
Orchards of mangoes and flowers galore;
The army paints murals on walls,
Songs of rejoicing are sung by all.

What beauty all around! Every corner of the kingdom dazzled, not with the glitter of jewels but with the radiant smiles of the people. Excitement filled the air as people hurried about, and sweets and treats were made by the dozen.

Amid all the feasting and revelry, under the glow of a beaming moon, the prince and princess circled a rosy red fire, declaring their love for one another and promising to always treat each other with respect and kindness. The fire, wind, birds, the forest, and its trees stood as witnesses to their vows. Cheers of merriment echoed all around.

One year passed, and then another. Gradually, time flew by, but the princess, who had left for her journey of exploration, was yet to return home. Her parents had nearly blinded themselves with tears, and the kingdom was in darkness. The people mourned.

One day, a to-do emerged. Drums at the entry gates began to be beaten at the break of dawn, and the gates trembled with the cries of horses, elephants, soldiers, and sentries.

Asked the queen, "What is happening?"

Asked the king, "Who is coming?"

Their darling princess was back! She had brought with her a young man as sweet as sugar. Mother and Father came trembling to welcome them in. No matter how often they hugged their daughter or held their son-in-law, their hearts wanted more.

The people sang the songs of joy.

The princess and her prince touched their golden sticks to the king and queen, vanquishing their blindness. All the grief in the land melted away at the touch of their magic wands.

After spending many happy and peaceful days with Mother and Father, they once again left to explore the world, hand in hand.

Who knows which other faraway land they would have to save with their magic touch?

Something to think about

Consent: *If you like someone, you can't just jump on them and show it. You have to try to understand whether they like you too. This understanding is called consent.*

The story of the story

The old version of this story is well known. The prince awakens a sleeping kingdom and finds his princess there, saving them all from a demon's curse. The princess is helpless, while the prince acts as the protector. The princess sleeps, and the prince travels. In our retelling, we have reversed the reasons for sleep, the identity of the sleeper and the savior, the helpless and the protector, and who plays what role throughout the kingdom.

Princess Kalawati

1

Once upon a time, there was a young princess named Kalawati, with hair as soft and fluffy as clouds. She sailed the river on her regal, bird-lipped barge, wrapped in silver and adorned with diamonds. With her was the golden Shuk bird, who loved to chat, but Kalawati seemed lost in thought, gazing at the shimmering waters as her barge drifted along.

Kalawati was on an adventure to see places and meet people. Crowds gathered on the riverbanks wherever her boat passed, whispering and pointing at her grand vessel.

"Who is she?" They wondered. "She must be important—a princess, perhaps! Look at her boat and that royal bird beside her!"

"*She has a vast country.*
The duties of which are manifold!
Kalawati is her name.
Like the queen of the world."

As the boat sailed further, it reached the edge of a new land. Something seemed different here. Kalawati frowned—*why were there guards at the gates? And who were those five sparkling women huddling by the riverbank?*

"They are the queens of this land," whispered the bird.

"All of them?" Kalawati asked, surprised.

"Yes," she said. "This land has one king who took seven queens. Two are in exile—one works at a zoo, and the other collects cow dung. They were sent away because they couldn't have sons."

Curious to know more, Kalawati was about to ask more when the five queens called out to her.

"Beautiful young lady with cloud-like hair,

Come take these pearl flowers, oh maiden fair."

the queens said, holding out sparkling bouquets.

But Kalawati smiled and said from her boat,

"Pearl flowers fill my chamber.

Past the kingdom of three old women, on the banks of the Ranga River."

Her boat sailed further down the river, and the queens called after her, curious.

"Which country's princess are you, and where is your land?

In marriage, give my moon-like son your pretty hand."

But by then, Kalawati's boat had floated too far away, and she replied with a laugh,

"Kalawati, I am the princess with cloud-like hair.

Send your son to Kalawati's lair."

And with that, her barge disappeared into the horizon.

They were excited by her challenge. The five queens sent word to their sons, who quickly saddled their winged horses and raced to inform their father, the king. Upon hearing of the mysterious princess, the king ordered five magnificent peacock-shaped *Mayurpankhi* ships to be prepared for the princes. They would embark on a journey across the world to find Kalawati and win her heart.

The adventure had only just begun!

2

On the other hand, Kalawati was listening to tales of the Dung-Collector Queen and the Zoo-Worker Queen as the evening sky turned orange.

"There was our king. He had seven queens, a great kingdom, a vast palace, elephants galore, and horses in stables. His treasury brimmed with jewels, and his royal crest shone on the doors. The kingdom was bustling with ministers, sepoys, soldiers, and courtiers.

But the king still had no joy or peace in his mind—none of his seven queens held a son in their arms. How would the kingdom get its heir if a son was not born? Now, imagine that! It was such a silly law of the land—only the son of a king could become a king.

Therefore, all the kingdom's people spent their days in gloom. The queens fell into great disgrace. They were held to blame."

Kalawati's surprise held no bounds. Her country was different. To be recognized as a leader by the country's people, one must pass various tests: a test of knowledge, a test of weaponry, a test of intellect, and a test of kindness and empathy. The leader could be either male or female. Therefore, Kalawati was surprised and said,

"The queens must have been so sad!"

"Sad and scared! The king could have their heads chopped off at any moment! Competition was also fierce. Everyone wanted to be the mother of a son! After all, the mother of a son today, Her Highness tomorrow."

"True!"

"One day, the queens went to bathe in the river. At that time, a monk showed up, gave a piece of root to the eldest queen, and said, 'Make a paste of this and eat it, all seven of you. You will be blessed with boys, marvelous as the moon.'"

"Then? What happened then?"

Shuk went on, "Hold your horses! After washing up, the queens first had to tend to the palace chores in clean clothes. Only then would they get a chance to make a paste of the root!"

"What?"

"The eldest would cook rice. The second would chop, the third would cook the dishes, the fourth fetched water, the fifth helped out, the sixth made the pastes, and the youngest one dressed the fish. Otherwise, the king would not eat!"

"The king didn't lift a finger then? Didn't even keep his own digestives?"

Don't you know! A husband's health comes from the cooking of the wife's hand—that's what they said in that strange country. So, five queens prevailed in the royal kitchen. Only the fourth queen went to draw water from the well, and the youngest queen sat down to scale and cut the fish. The eldest queen had the monk's root. She instructed the sixth queen that it should be pasted before the spices. Everyone ate a little. In order of seniority, everyone ate a little bit—eldest, second, third, fifth. The fourth queen got the scrapings, and the youngest, only the water used to wash the grindstone.

"Dear me!"

"The whole incident reached the king's ears. He thought that even if the fourth and youngest queens had sons, they would surely be defective."

"What brains! As if eating a root ensures having sons!"

"But ensure it did! Ten months and ten days passed. All seven queens had boys. But the king's mind was still not at ease. In the meantime, the boys grew like the moon.

"The king kept a watch—were the sons born to the fourth and youngest deformed in any way? Ultimately, he asked his minister to find out. On the day of their coming-of-age ceremony, the minister passed on his duty to the priest."

"What did he say?"

"He said that the youngest queen's son was not very masculine. He didn't fight like his brothers. Of course, he jumped and ran about. But he had a gentle gait with a rhythmic grace—a beat. There was no aggression in him. He was named Buddhu."

"As if it's a bad thing to have a rhythmic gait!"

"There's more. The priest said the fourth queen's son was less intelligent than other boys his age. He was named Bhutum. The king thought his fear had come true! What will he do with these defective princes? Would they not make him lose his glory?"

Kalawaticuppedhercheeksandwidenedhereyestilltheyreachedherforehead. "Stone-hearted father!"

"The other queens also gave their input, 'These two boys are the disgrace of the clan.'" This would reduce two claimants to the throne. Their sons were given fancy names: Heera, the dazzling diamond; Manik, the remarkable ruby; Moti, the prodigious pearl; Shankha, the incredible coral; and Kanchan, the glistening gold. The king shooed away the fourth queen and youngest queen from the palace. The fourth queen became a worker at the zoo, and the youngest one began to collect dung.

Tears rolled from Kalawati's eyes. Shuk went on, "Five princes rode about on their five-winged horses with many attendants and guards by their side! Bhutum and Buddhu relaxed on the branches of the Bakul tree near the mothers' huts and sang songs. Their five brothers would hit someone on one day and behead someone else the next. The people of the kingdom were extremely annoyed by their antics. Bhutum and Buddhu played sports, sang, danced, and helped their mothers. Buddhu collected dung. Bhutum lovingly fed the birds in the aviary. Sometimes, they went to the forest on the south of the palace. Budhhu collected flowers for the mothers. Bhutum brought them betel nuts for their betel leaves."

"So, they were quite happy, weren't they, Shuk?"

"They were. But one day, the five princes came to visit the zoo. They caught Buddhu and Bhutum without saying a word and dragged them to the palace. The whims of princes! Their mothers wept bitterly. But the hearts of the princes did not melt.

"Buddhu and Bhutum were wide-eyed at the splendor of the palace. But the old sentries recognized them and bowed down. The old maids said, 'Aren't they the sons of the fourth and youngest queens?'

"The five princes did not know about their other two mothers. Once they learned, they, too, shooed Buddhu and Bhutum away. While they ran away, they also came to learn of their true identities. With their heads held high, they arrived at the royal court before the king. The doorkeeper recognized them and stood aside. The ministers roared in rage. Buddhu and Bhutum jumped straight into the arms of the king and addressed him as "father." The king's eyes began to water. He pulled the boys and held them to his chest. But I can't tell you what happened after that."

Kalawati said, "Oh no! Why? Tell me, please!?"

Said Shuk,

"*I can read past and present.*
But the future is something other than what I know.
Sweet are the fruits of patience,
This is an important lesson.
May Kalawati, her companion, get
No more tears nor reason to fret."

3

Meanwhile, the atmosphere in the palace was one of grandeur and elegance. Five Mayurpankhi ships raised their flags. The queens ululated as their sons ascended the boats and headed for Kalawati's land.

The king also arrived at the banks of the river with Buddhu and Bhutum in tow. They asked, "Father, what goes there?"

"Mayurpankhi, peacock ships."

"Where do they go?"

"To the land of the Princess Kalawati."

"We want to go too. Give us Mayurpankhi ships, too."

The queens began to chirp.

"Who's that? Who's that? The son of the zoo maid? The son of the dung collector?"

The princes laughed out loud, and the king was embarrassed. Fearing public shame, he abandoned his sons again. The king and the queens returned to the palace.

Buddhu-Bhutum cried a lot. Then Buddhu said, "Dada, let's go to the carpenter's shop. We'll also get peacock ships made. We will go where our brothers went."

Bhutum said, "Let's go."

Buddhu and Bhutum did not return home for three days. Their mothers were full of grief and fear. When they heard the princes would bring the princess from the faraway land, they wept because of their misfortune. They came to the riverside crying. They floated two vermillion-dotted betel leaves with rice and *durba* grass wrapped within. They sang,

"*Buddhu-Bhutum, our kin,*
What has been our sin?
Why have you left us with so much regret?
Where the bird-shaped boat goes, peacock ships follow.
Had you been true sons, you would go in this canoe."

Saying this, they floated their betel leaf canoes and returned to the hut.

Meanwhile, on the way to the carpenter's house, Bhutum and Buddhu saw two betel leaf boats floating away. Buddhu said, "Wow, Dada, let's climb aboard these two boats."

The two brothers sat in the two canoes, which floated near the peacock ships. People turned their noses in disgust.

"What on earth is this?" They asked.

Buddhu-Bhutum said, "We are Buddhu and Bhutum."

Laughter rang out loud from the Mayurpankhi ships.

Remember that Kalawati had said her home was "*Past the kingdom of three old women, on the banks of the Ranga River*"? The three old women were her three demoness maternal aunts. Of course, they were her guardians, too. The three sisters lived happily in the same land. But they had a habit of swallowing alive any strange human they saw. It was evening when the Mayurpankhi ships of the five princes landed on their riverbanks. The old women came stomping their sticks to see the guests, with their white hair blowing like jute.

The princes were full of pride. Why should they talk to these old hags? Prince Heera said, "Hey you, we are princes. Go and tell your king that we have arrived. We wish to stay here for the night."

The first old woman said, "If you want something, you must bow down first, son. Why do you show off such arrogance?"

Prince Shankha said, "Just hear what this woman says! Why should we speak to beggars? We'd still consider it if you were a courtier or soldier. Aren't there guards by the river in your land?"

The second old woman said, "We three old ladies are the guards."

Her words made the princes fall about with laughter. Prince Manik said,

"What does the old woman say? Women guards! That too, these women with their ancient bones!"

The old women then revealed their true identities. They spun their sticks this way and that. Soldiers and courtiers rushed forward, but their swords fell to the ground due to the blows from their sticks. In the blink of an eye, they all found themselves bound by ropes, and the old women took them to their kingdom. Then? The third old woman said, "Sister, arrangements for our meals for three full days!"

They were as good as their word. For three days, one by one, they swiftly ate all the people in ropes. By the third evening, sailors, oarsmen, soldiers, courtiers, princes—all had been eaten clean! But how strange—they were not digested. The women's stomachs contained a vast prison. The princes had to stay there, crammed with sweaty bodies and corpses. They felt disgusted. They wanted to cry. They had never even stayed in the servant's rooms! They snapped at the sailors and rowers, "Hey you, move away!"

The sailors whispered amongst themselves, "Look at their brains! They're drenched in drool, bathed in bile—but they find our sweat more repulsive!"

The princes said, "Brothers, we'll be in these old women's stomachs for the rest of our lives. We won't get to see our mothers or father again."

On the other hand, the betel leaf boats reached the river banks three days later. The three old women arrived with the prison in their stomachs. Buddhu saw them and touched his head to the ground in a gesture of respect. He asked one of them, "Grandmother, your land is so beautiful! There are so many flowers and so many trees! It is green all over. Even this moonlit darkness looks so green! There is a similar jungle near our hutments, too. We brothers live there with our two unfortunate mothers."

Bhutum grew busy with the island's nocturnal birds. He looked for the birds that he used to feed at the aviary. The three old women took a liking to the two gentle boys and invited them to take shelter in their kingdom.

While speaking to the grand ladies, Buddhu and Bhutum learned their brothers were imprisoned within their stomachs. Bhutum lovingly stroked their white hair. Buddhu cooked all the delicacies he had learned from his mother for them. After many requests, the old women freed the princes with all their retinue. "Hey, hey, ho-yak!"

Instantly, the five princes and their sailors, rowers, soldiers, and courtiers emerged from their stomachs, covered in vomit and bile–yikes! The old witches took them to the river banks. The princes bathed and cleaned themselves and then ordered the sails to be lifted. No one inquired about Buddhu or Bhutum. Once again, they sailed alongside on their betel leaf boats.

The Mayurapankhi ships ran all night and reached the Ranga River in the morning. The river had neither source nor edge, only red water. The sailors lost their way. Everyone started to panic. Seven days and seven nights. It seemed that the ships would go down at any moment. The princes said, "Alas! Buddhu would have saved us for sure."

Just then, Buddhu-Bhutum appeared in their betel-leaf canoe.

"*What brother, what brother?*

What do you want, what do you want?"

They came up after tying the canoe to two peacock feathers. Buddhu looked around and said, "Set sail to the north."

Gradually, they went down the river and came to the edge of a mango-jackfruit tree. The starving princes ate the fruit, which calmed them down. They then said, "Why are these beggars in our peacock ships? Throw them both in the water."

The sailors threw Budhu-Bhutum and their two canoes into the water. The Mayupankhis moved on.

But karma cannot be escaped! As they continued, they were caught in a whirlpool, and all the five peacocks, along with the princes, sailors, and courtiers aboard, were drawn in. Not a trace of them remained.

After some time, Buddhu and Bhutum's canoes came there. Buddhu said, "Brother, something does not bode well. What happened here? Let's dive in and see."

Bhutum said, "Damn them! Only if they die can we live in peace! Ungrateful monsters."

Buddhu said, "No, don't say that. You stay. I have tied a thread around my waist. When I pull on it, lift me. Not before that."

Saying this, Buddhu dived in. Bhutum sat holding the thread.

Descending through the waters, Buddhu reached the land of the underground. There was a big tunnel, which he crossed and reached the gate of a royal kingdom. A hundred-year-old old woman sat there and sewed *Nakshi Kantha* quilts. Her quilt had on it two vibrant, life-like girls. One danced while the other fought. The old woman asked, "Which of the two designs do you like? Tell me?"

Buddhu saw the loom woven so that the left part of the warrior's face and the right part of the dancer's face were visible. They were the same girl.

He firmly said,

"When harsh and mild come as one
Only then can be sung a duet.
Why choose sides of a coin,
Both are good. Both correct."

The old woman then said, "Is that so? A lot it is that you seem to know! Tell me, whose picture is this?"

Buddhu said, "None other than Kalawati."

"Five had come before you. They said, 'One is Kalawati; who knows what kind of witch the other one is?' Insulting women is a grave offense in our land. Those five are now behind bars."

Saying this, the old woman let Buddhu in. He entered the royal kingdom, where Kalawati was holding court. The five princes were brought in, their hands and feet chained up. Their crime was that they had insulted warrior women. The commander had laughed at the girl. Their minister had made fun. However, Kalawati had also deployed a lawyer to speak on their behalf. Criminals also had the right to speak in this country. The lawyer said, "They did not know any better! Their country is strange and silly. It is customary there to degrade girls."

Kalawati was so angry at hearing this that she immediately wanted to declare war against their land. Biting back her words, she said with great difficulty, "Send them to the mental sanatorium. Let them learn from scratch."

"Before that, forget what you have learned," said the minister.

The commander said, "Two hard blows and all mislearning will be wiped clean."

The courtiers laughed out loud, "I guess they deserve those things too! What do you call them? Hmmm . . . Oh yes, human rights!"

Debate erupted in the court. It was decided that the outcome would be voted upon.

Suddenly, Prince Heera cried out, "Buddhu, my brother, Iron strikes on my golden skin! I can't bear it any longer!"

The eyes of the entire royal court turned toward the enormous curtains. A new arrival was meekly standing behind them. His hands were folded, his eyes downcast. The sepoy women caught him and brought him in front of Kalawati.

She asked, "Five men were expected. Who are you, pray?"

Buddhu said, "The ashes of the Dung-Collector Queen."

Tears welled up in Kalawati's eyes. After all, she had just recently heard the tragic tale of the two queens on her journey! She asked, "Where is your brother?"

"He is sitting on the betel leaf boat, holding onto the thread tied around my waist."

Kalawati then sent her people, who climbed up the thread and warmly invited Bhutum back to the castle.

Kalawati said, "You have traveled from a faraway land and crossed many hurdles on your way here. Stay here for a while."

Buddhu said, "We wish to take our brothers and return home."

"That cannot be done," Kalawati said. "They must be educated first. They must learn home-making, how to sew and knit, how to love, and master pity and compassion. That will take as long as it takes. Only if they pass will they be allowed to go home."

Buddhu-Bhutum said, "Then let us stay, too. We can't leave them here after all! Bonds of blood. But the mothers will be so upset! Can they be sent word?"

"So be it."

Kalawati ended court for the day.

Grand arrangements were made for their stay. But no one simply existed in that kingdom—everyone worked. So Buddhu became the court poet, and Bhutum a chef. Women left their children in the nursery when they went to work. Bhutum began to cook simple, nutritious meals without spice for the children. And he, who loved birds so much, became best friends with Shuk!

A year passed in this manner. The five princes were aghast—they kept failing again and again. Each time, their classes began anew. Buddhu-Bhutum spent their days happily. After he was done with work for the day, Bhutum rode Shuk's back and traveled around the land. After court ended for the day, Buddhu and Kalawati went out together to the gardens and forests of the land. They discussed poetry sometimes and politics at other times. He picked fruits and berries from the trees for Kalawati, just like he used to for the mothers. Kalawati liked both his small gifts and his gentle nature. Then, when the sky and air were awash with spring colors, Buddhu mustered courage and shyly gave Kalawati flowers instead of fruits. The red *kingshuk* flowers. Kalawati, too, accepted them bashfully. Through this exchange, the two got married within their hearts without uttering a single word. Once they returned, Kalawati announced that Buddhu would be her lifelong companion.

Excitement descended over the kingdom. Drums started beating. Decorations were prepared and arrangements made, and the wedding day arrived quickly. On that day, a Mayurpankhi ship arrived right in front of the palace gates. Everyone's heart skipped a beat. The doors of the boat, however, did not open. The vessel was from Jagatpuri, and it had a royal lion crest. The five princes had come on such ships! Then, had their kingdom sent an army? But how did they cross the kingdom of the three old women? Would there be a war now? The troops rushed to the armory. What was going on? On a day meant for celebration, they were now preparing for war!

Just then, the doors of the ship opened. The king himself descended, along with his five queens. He took Kalawati's hands in his own and said, "We, too, have arrived so we can learn anew—so that all our sins may be washed away. Will there be a place for us?"

Saying so, the mighty king burst into tears.

Everyone in Kalawati's kingdom had tears in their eyes. The minister cried. The sentry wailed. Our Kalawati, too, was awash. But Buddhu and Bhutum's eyes seemed to be searching for someone.

Suddenly, Shuk came and sat on Bhutum's shoulder and said,

"Brother Bhutum, Brother Bhutum,
Have no fear!
Kalawati's two more mothers-in-law,
Look! They come near."

Budhhu and Bhutum looked up and exclaimed, "Ma!"

Their grieving, long-suffering mothers had arrived too!

They take turns hugging each other and weeping—what a unique sight! Amid all this happy bustle, Buddhu and Kalawati were married.

Then?

After three years of training in Kalawati's kingdom, the five princes, five queens, and the king returned to their land on their Mayurpankhi ships with their soldiers, courtiers, and guards. But the two neglected queens stayed on in the new land. Although the king made innumerable requests and the queens tried to reason with them often, they did not agree to return. Here, they taught teach music and dance. They raised the children in the royal nursery. They were much happier.

Buddhu-Bhutum, too, stayed behind in this new land. Bhutum became the Minister of Animal Husbandry, and Buddhu was appointed the Minister of Arts and Culture. Tales of their virtues spread by word of mouth. They became examples of the many virtues men could possess beyond wielding swords and flexing their muscles.

Meanwhile, don't ask me what is happening in the kingdom of Jagatpuri! They are rectifying themselves, making mistakes again, and then correcting themselves. Who knows, maybe one day they will be fully fixed!

SOMETHING TO THINK ABOUT

Different qualities within men: *Our Buddhu and Bhutum do not love fighting. They avoid displays of power or brute force unnecessarily. They enjoy poetry and cooking for their mothers and the three grandmothers. They like to bring fruits for their mothers and Kalawati. Bhutum also loves animals. Buddhu is anxious to save his brothers despite their cruelty toward him. This is the kind of man Kalawati falls in love with, showing that a boy does not necessarily have to become an instrument of violence—he can choose to pursue his desires through kindness rather than seizing them through force.*

THE STORY OF THE STORY

This famous story is named 'Kalawati' *in the book* 'Thakumar Jhuli'. *The esteemed Bengali singers Hemanta Mukhopadhyay, Kazi Sabyasachi, Asha Devi, and Sandhya Mukhopadhyay came together to create an audio recording based on this story, named "Buddhu-Bhutum". In the story of "Kalawati", Kalawati is little more than just a reward. Buddhu-Bhutum and the five princes compete to win her. Kalawati has hardly any story of her own. It was the story of Buddhu-Bhutum's expedition. The story begins with their birth and ends with their accession to the throne and transformation. What about Kalawati?*

When I wrote this story again, I started with Kalawati's expedition. I gave her a country of her own, a court, a council, and a lot of dialogue. But Bhutum and Buddhu remained; their expedition remained. You are now the best judges of how this new story turned out.

Kanchanmala, Kakanmala

1

Kanchanmala and Kakanmala were friends and playmates. Kanchanmala was pretty and had many talents. She belonged to the royal family. Kakanmala, a farmer's daughter, neither had the looks, skills, or qualities worthy of praise; nor was she beautiful like the girls in the fairy stories. Her most considerable wealth in life was her friendship with Kanchanmala.

Kakanmala would have to cook and pack lunch for her father and take it to him while he toiled in the fields, whereas, at the palace, Kanchanmala trained in music and dance; she was also good with paint and brush and even knew how to prepare the most regal meals (which she learned from her mother, the queen herself). "Virtues such as those that you are picking up so well, my dear, make a woman virtuous," the queen would say. Later, the two friends would embrace each other, sit under the shade of the trees, and talk about their hearts' desires. That was how their days went by.

Like the moon, they grew up bit by bit. Kanchanmala was married off to become the queen of another kingdom. Her treasure chests overflowed with precious gems and jewels. She had servants galore to attend to her every need. How could she, a queen, even remember some farmer's daughter from her childhood? How could she even consider someone like her a friend? Soon Kanchanmala forgot Kakanmala.

Kanchanmala's husband, the king, was not a very people-friendly as a ruler. The poor were forbidden to enter his palace. Slowly, the arrogance within him transferred to Kanchanmala, too.

One day, Kakanmala staged a demonstration in front of the palace doors. "The queen and I used to play with dolls together!" she said. The queen grimaced when she heard, and the guards shooed Kakanmala away. No one knows where she went from there, with all that pain in her heart.

2

The next day, Queen Kanchanmala woke to find the king in distress. His face, entire body, and even his hair were full of needles! Wails erupted across the kingdom, and the people began to mourn.

But how had this happened? The royal physician came to see the king but did not have any answers. Only Kanchanmala knew in her heart that our consciences prick when we commit misdeeds. Was this the result of ignoring that poor woman, her former friend, Kakanmala?

The kingdom of the Needle King came to a standstill. The king sat with his head bowed low in despair. Queen Kanchanmala began to take over the reins of the kingdom to the best of her ability.

Kanchanmala consults the minister, and ultimately, both decide to hold a council of learned priests. These wise scholars made calculations and said,

"*The king and queen, though once so grand,*
Must now face poverty hand in hand.
The people's judgment, cold and stern,
A lesson in humility to learn.
But if they feel regret, sincere,
And ask for forgiveness, drawing near—
With folded hands, their pride laid low,
Only then will mercy grow."

The queen then left in search of her old friend. They met in their old village, under the shade of the old tree where they would once sit. Kakanmala was now the wife of a cowherd.

The two embraced each other just like in the old days and cried for some time. Kakanmala then said that her husband was distraught, too. In his childhood, he had been the playmate of the Needle King. The king had forgotten him, just like his queen had forgotten Kakanmala.

Kanchanmala held her hands to her ears to ask for forgiveness. She gave Kakanmala all her jewelry and a beautiful silk saree. While shedding tears and

begging for forgiveness, she asked for the coarse nine-yard cloth Kakanmala wore. After all, she had to begin living the life of a peasant.

After many requests, the cowherd and cowherdess agreed to accompany the queen to the palace. The cowherd played his flute as he walked. Behind him was Kakanmala, dressed like a royal queen. Kanchanmala, shivering in the winter cold in her cotton saree, brought up the rear.

3

Kakanmala began to change after entering the palace, adopting the airs and graces of a queen. She had never seen such splendor before, nor had she ever enjoyed such power. For the first time in her life, horses and elephants lay drained in front of her; she didn't even have to set foot on uncarpeted floors. She started to become very arrogant. The cowherd, too, needed to remember the simple tunes of his flute. Neither of them went anywhere near the old king.

Kanchanmala, on the other hand, survived on leftovers—fermented *panta* rice with small *mourola* fish. She sat by piles of scales and fish heads as she gutted her fish and washed her own clothes. She caressed her hand against her husband's head. The poor Needle King lived in constant agony from the needles constantly pricking him—an agony so excruciating that one wouldn't wish it even on their worst enemy.

The royal priests observed that the situation was dire. The cowherd and cowherdess were as pleasure-loving as the king and the queen. After consulting, they declared that Kakanmala would have to feed the king *pithe* by hand on the auspicious winter solstice day. No, not fancy royal delicacies like *Chandrapuli*, *Mohan Bashi*, or *Kheer Murali*—he had eaten enough of those! Queen Kanchanmala was a master at making them, too. The king had never tasted the winter sweets made in farmers' homes—*Aaske*, *Chaaske*, and *Ghaaske*. And only Kakanmala knew how to make them. Perhaps eating this sweet, made by an ordinary woman, would wipe the king's sins away. The cowherd could also play for him the songs of harvest he had long forgotten.

Preparations were made accordingly. Kakan ground rice and made Aaske in clay pots in a humble oven. The cowherd chopped down branches of a tree to get the freshest *Nolen* jaggery. On the auspicious day, Kakanmala and the cowherd, led by Kanchanmala, went to the king's room.

When they entered, they stopped in their tracks—what was this they could see?

Scores of flies buzzing around,
the agony of a thousand wounds,
Poorer than the poorest,
His suffering knows no rest.
Once such a mighty king,
Royally punished he has been!

Kakan and the cowherd's eyes welled with tears, and fear crept into their minds. Did splendor and arrogance lead to such a dreadful fate? Kakan threw her jewels off and flung them to the ground.

The cowherd began to play his flute—out rolled a sweet, simple tune from their childhood. Kakanmala first fed the king some *Aaske pithe* and then her old friend Kanchan. Kanchanmala had never eaten a sweet so simple yet so soft and delicious.

The scent of newly churned jaggery filled the room. With flies buzzing around, the king went straight to the bowl with the leftover pithe. What do you think happened next?

The moment the king's friend forgave him, the needles began to fall off his body. His mind and body did not sting anymore.

Peals of excitement broke out across the kingdom. Little boys and girls ran to the palace to paint *alpona* on this auspicious day. Some drew lotus flowers, *shaluk* vines, and rice paddy with ground rice grains. Others drew peacocks, dolls, and birds of all shapes and colors. All of them coated their hands in paint and printed their palms, creating a beautiful map of a hundred handprints—a map to a place where everyone was an individual, and yet no one was alone. A single image had been born out of the hundred prints—no one could tell which print belonged to a king and which belonged to a cowherd.

The king said, "Friend, don't think ill of me. Please don't leave me and go."

The queen, too, said, "Dear friend, don't think me ill. Please don't leave me and go."

Kakanmala replied, "Why don't you ask the guards to remove the walls instead? If the walls come down, I will be where you are, and our differences will melt away."

Kakanmala's idea was immediately implemented. The walls that separated the king and the courtier were brought down. After finishing their work for the day, the king and cowherd spent their evenings beneath the shade of a tree. The cowherd played raga *Yaman*, and the king took lessons from him.

These days, you'd find Kanchanmala and Kakanmala in the forest right next to the kingdom. With their sarees hitched up to their knees, they sit by the pond and dip their legs in the water of a pond. Don't ask me what tales they exchange with each other and why they collapse into giggles after every few minutes! Those are the secrets of girlhood.

SOMETHING TO THINK ABOUT

Breaking down walls: *The king and the cowherd, the queen and the farmer's daughter—the same red blood flows through each of their veins. On the other hand, the king and queen, the cowherd and cowherdess, despite some being women and others being men, are all human beings, aren't they? Then why are there so many invisible walls between people in our world?*

The pricking of the needles: When we feel bad after doing something wrong, it is said that our conscience is pricking us. Have you ever felt like this? Does your conscience prick as much as a needle?

THE STORY OF THE STORY

The old story is based on two different materials. In the first, a king is punished for neglecting his friend, who is a cowherd, and this friend saves him later. In the second, we meet "good girl" Kanchanmala and "bad girl" Kakanmala, highlighting the differences between them. The bad girl cannot make fancy pithes; she can only make the ones usually made in farmers' homes. She is depicted as greedy and a cheat, while the good girl knows how to make the most elaborate pithes and restore her husband to his previous healthy, happy self. The good and bad girls were never friends.

We kept the message of friendship from the first source material but doubled it. But we mixed up who the good girl was and who the bad girl was. They both had goodness within them; both were a little bad, courageous and a little helpless—just like us.

Seven Brothers Champa

1

There was one lone king with not one but six queens. After all, they said the king was entitled to his whims and fancies! He could simply marry every woman he took a liking to. Of course, there was a need for an heir; that was a reason, too. But as Lady Luck would have it, none of the six queens of our story had even one baby. The king asked the priests and astrologers, who reviewed charts and horoscopes and kept recommending more queens—the king should take in maidens with sparkling charts and no one else. But alas! The royal palace didn't trill with the pitter-patter of tiny feet.

The king may keep marrying, but could he love all his wives equally? They were forever competing with each other for the king's attention and affection. Amidst all that, the old king took a liking to another young maiden. The royal priest approved, saying that she was indeed a fortune-fair. She complained about nothing and never raised her voice; wasn't she truly worthy of being the king's consort? Who knows, perhaps she would be the one to produce the royal heir? The king immediately dispatched his men to send for the maiden. They got married, and the palace got its seventh queen.

The six older queens smelled danger. They were convinced that it was only time before the king would forget all about them. But their lips parted to speak nothing but the sweetest of words. Their nose rings twinkled, bangled and tinkled as they prepared to welcome the newest queen.

The youngest queen became a captive in the palace. Before, she had lived at the eastern edge of the royal mango and jackfruit orchards. Not used to fancy meals nor jewelry chests brimming with silver and gold, she enjoyed the open sky above her head and the freedom of roaming the entire jungle, which felt as if it belonged to only her. She had grown up with the trees and plants, birds, and beasts of the wild. But now, it was time for all that running free, exploring, and unchecked movement to stop. In the palace, the young queen befriended a servant named Moti. She poured her heart out to her.

Moti, in turn, reported all of the young queen's woes to the six older queens. They began to whisper amongst themselves,

"My dear friend,
Look how caught in the king's trap
A koi fish wriggles to its end.
Wrong were we to speak ill of her, our gossip must end.
We share the same woes; after all, an ear to her we must lend.
Why do we stay far apart when we can make a friend?"

One afternoon, the six queens, lavishly chewing the betel wraps prepared by their servants, came to befriend the young queen. She was pleased to have found six new friends. She informed them that the king was now just too old to be able to have any children. Thus, it was just a matter of time before someone else would take her place. The seven queens began to plan a solution.

That afternoon, Moti informed the sentries that the queens were discussing the *Putra Yajna*, a prayer ritual for sons. Everyone was forbidden from entering the queens' quarters.

Do you know what they were up to? They were deep in discussion, but not about how to have a son. Then?

Stop! That's not for you to know just yet.

The fruits of patience are lovely indeed.

2

Three days later, news reached the king that the youngest queen was expecting a son. The king's joy knew no bounds. For an entire week, he distributed money and gifts to the poor of the kingdom. He also released prisoners who had been waiting for years in the royal prison for justice. News of the king's bout of benevolence spread across the kingdom. Hearing this, the queens laughed amongst themselves.

The king was overjoyed that he would be getting an heir soon. But don't think for a moment that he set aside his own work or pleasures and spent his time caring for the youngest queen! He was a busy man, after all. If he stayed near the youngest queen the whole day or showed too much concern about her, people might call him a "henpecked husband"! So, the king had a set of golden chains made. He tied one end around the youngest queen's waist and the other to his own. The queen was ordered to shake the shackles and inform the king only when she gave birth to a son. He would come with scholars and priests to meet his son for the first time at an auspicious hour.

But who would stay in the birthing room? The other queens said, "The first royal heir is to be born; we will stay there ourselves." Thus, the remaining six queens were given the responsibility for the delivery. They said it was essential to keep the youngest queen safe now; she had to be protected from the evil eye! They asked the king to dismiss all the servants from there except for a few trustworthy maids. The king explained to all the palace staff their responsibilities in the upcoming days and then returned to his royal court. The queens let out sighs of relief—precisely what they had wanted.

They thought they could be at ease for ten months and ten days. They oiled and braided each other's hair, laughed, and gossiped. The eldest queen, who loved to paint, brought out her easel, brushes, and colors.

The second queen always wished to wear gems and beads from many foreign lands. She focused her attention on making strings to wear around her neck. The third queen fulfilled her desire to ride free on horseback. The fourth queen was the best of the best in archery. She got to string her bow with arrows after a long time.

The fifth queen sang out loud to her heart's content. And the sixth queen, who was a talented dancer, began to give lessons to the attendant maids. It seemed like a festival raged in the queens' quarters. The queens felt as if they were breathing free after years.

What about the youngest queen? She loved plants and animals. Countless flowers bloomed under her care. She had the concrete floors broken down, allowing the soil to come through and be nourished with fertilizer and water. Parul flowers began to blossom, and Champa flowers laughed a giddy laugh—she had created something as beautiful as the gardens of heaven. Birds came to eat grain from the queen's hand, and stray cats and dogs found a home that sheltered them.

The queens no longer bickered. Instead, they often gave each other pecks on the cheek, combed their hair, and lived happily to their heart's content.

3

Nine months passed. The king did not come near the queens' quarters. He had somewhat forgotten about them. What use did he have for them after all? His heir was almost here! The queens, too, were content amongst themselves. But their days in the sun were drawing to a close. What would they tell the king when there would be no heir? They couldn't come up with an answer.

One day, Moti arrived with devastating news—the kingdom's farmers would be beheaded for not being able to pay royal taxes! They had been brought to the court bound in chains. The youngest queen's poor father was amongst them too! The queens began to moan loudly, and the youngest queen beat her breast and said,

"*I had a father, though he lived afar,*
Throughout my childhood, he was my guiding star,
How do I save him? What do I do?
If his life ends—I will end mine too."

The eldest queen came up with the solution; she asked the youngest queen to lie down and rang the golden bell.

The chain around the king's waste began to shake on the other side of the palace. Immediately, he thought that a strapping young son must have been born to his youngest queen. He dismissed the court instantly. The minister asked, "What about punishing the farmers, your majesty?"

"All sentences will be remitted, and all taxes will be waived. The royal prince has been born!"

The king called his priests and scholars. Drums and trumpets began to play with great aplomb. The palace was decorated like never before. The king led a grand procession to meet his son for the first time.

The queens were at sea. Yes, they had rung the bell to prevent the king from meting out a harsh sentence. But now that he was on his way, how would they produce a son? The youngest queen sat on the bed, her eyes red from crying. The six queens held her and hugged her from both sides. The seven sisters were intertwined even as they started shaking.

4

"Where is the newborn?" The king came and asked.

The queens pointed.

A cat and a dog that the youngest queen had given shelter to in the past, had given birth that very day. The king saw that the queens were pointing in their direction.

The gems and jewels in the king's hands fell to the floor. The drums stopped beating, and trumpets no longer played. The faces of the priests and scholars were ashen. The king's eyes burned like a thousand fires. Had the youngest queen given birth to kittens and puppies after everything? He dragged her by the hair and threw her out of the kingdom. Moti followed.

The six queens bravely said, "Does only the womb shape the child to be born? Does the father have no role in it?"

The king could not believe his ears. The audacity! The cheek! He immediately ordered the six queens banished, and their maids followed them. The royal palace was almost devoid of women. Dogs and cats went after the queens. The trees? The flowers? The Champas? The Paruls? Well, they couldn't move. They are tied to the ground. They bent their heads low and didn't raise them again.

Crossing the river and scaling the mountain, the seven queens built a new family with animals and birds. Flowers bloomed again. Besides the maids, other women from the kingdom, who had also been spending their days in misery, joined them. The rough land became green with their love.

5

But in the king's kingdom, darkness prevailed. The land was empty. Flowers did not bloom in the garden, and birds didn't call. The king thought spring did not come into his kingdom because there was no daily worship!

One day, the gardener said, "Maharaj, seven beautiful Champas and one beautiful Parul have sprouted today."

The king said, "What a surprise! Why have you still not brought flowers? Bring them now. Let me perform my puja."

The gardener said, "I can't do that!"

The king said, "Why?"

Then, the gardener gave a surprising explanation. The Parul flower was giving instructions to the Champas, which they obeyed! The more the gardener reached for them, the more Parul says,

"*Wake up, Champas, my brothers seven!*
Sister Parul calls you. Have a listen.

We don't mind the gardener, but the flower owner we hate,
Falling into his hands cannot be our fate."

Saying this, the eight flowers gradually went up and said,

"Come first in royal clothes,
Then we will discuss cons and pros."

So, the poor gardener got scared and nervous, threw his basket, and ran to tell the news.

Surprised, the king took his councilors to see what was going on.

6

The moment that the king tried to pluck a flower upon his arrival, the Parul flower said,

"Wake up, Champas, my brothers seven!
Sister Parul calls you. Have a listen.
Does the king these flowers own?
Can we let him take them home?"

The seven Champas answered,

"No, no, not a single flower will get he
He must swear never to cut any tree!"

The king swore.

Immediately, the Champas chorused again,

"Not a single flower will he get
He makes the farmers woe and fret!"

The king immediately gave his cultivators their fair share of the yielded crop. He wanted the flowers badly; he had to perform his puja after all!

But the moment he extended his hand toward the flowers again, they chimed,

"No, no, not a single flower will get he,
He shooed away his seven queens, as cruel as can be!"

The king then sent the best ministers and nobles to bring the queens honorably back to the kingdom. They went and threw themselves at the queens' feet. Their hearts melted. Oh! There was no yield in the state, no green! In due time, it would become as barren as a desert. The queens got up on the royal carriages to return to the kingdom and make flowers bloom again.

7

The carriage stood in the garden where the Champas and Parul bloomed. The six queens and all the maids made way for the youngest queen. Her hands could grow flora of all colors, shapes, and sizes; she was the mother of flowers. The youngest queen said nothing; she smiled softly and looked at the flowers. The seven brothers Champa and one sister, Parul, jumped into her lap, crying, "Ma, our dearest, Ma!"

Tears welled in the eyes of the ministers and councilors. Tears shone in the eyes of the people, too. The animals and birds who returned also had tears in their eyes. Tears fell fast, even from the king's eyes. He placed the youngest queen on the throne. He put the crown on her head. He gave the scepter to her hand. He assigned the duties of the kingdom and the subjects to the queens. Then, he went to the forest in a state of absolute calmness.

The birds sing on both sides of the mountain, and the flowers whisper. Their fragrance blends in the sky. Perhaps that scent reaches far away, into the forest, and mellows even the king's mind.

SOMETHING TO THINK ABOUT

We share the same woes, after all! The seven queens are shown to face the same problems. So why are they initially jealous of each other? Don't you often see in fairy tales that the queens fight among themselves about who will be a son's mother first and who will be the king's favorite? Why does this happen in all stories? What do you think? The source of the idea is in this new story itself! Try to find it out.

The mother of trees, mother of flowers, the mother of dogs and cats—who is a mother? When we say "Mother," do we all understand the same thing? Is the one whose chest heaves with affection the true mother? Whether you are a boy or a girl, maybe you are someone's mother! Aren't you the mother of your pet dog? Or the Krishnachura tree? Or the beautiful green parrot? Or a beggar on the road?

THE STORY OF THE STORY

"Saat Bhai Champa" is a prevalent folk tale. In it, the jealous six elder queens kill the youngest queen's seven children and bury them in the ground. The king is shown the litter of dogs and cats and told that they are the children of Chhoto Rani. There is a lot of cruelty hidden in fairy tales, as in this story.

However, the youngest queen's dead children blossom into flowers. They report the exploits of the six elder queens to the king. But while writing our story, we see that the beginning needs to be revised. If the king is desperate for a child and marries seven times, then every new queen will be determined to be the mother of the royal heir.

In this new story, we gave the queens some peace and a means of survival other than their children.

Prince Red Lotus, Prince Blue Lotus

1

People whispered that one of the two queens of the kingdom was no human. She sneaked off to the elephant stables and feasted on them. The horses, too. If you hear this, you'll scoff and say it's untrue. Then the people will say, "She's a demon! She's capable of many strange, wicked things."

But in reality, the younger queen just loved to eat. All day long, she thought about food. So, people said that she was a demoness—why else would her mouth seem to be watering all day??

The other queen was holy. She didn't eat at all! Eating was a sign of gluttony and greed. It wasn't acceptable for women to be greedy!

The two queens had two boys: Kusum, the elder queen's son, and Ajit, the younger queen's son. The two brothers were best of friends.

The holy queen abstained from food and grew as thin as a reed. She became bedridden and, one day, died in the blink of an eye.

People said the younger queen had been salivating—indeed, she must have killed off her co-wife!

Kusum was a soft-hearted boy who broke down. But Ajit was quite the opposite—as tough as iron. He wiped Kusum's tears and took care of him. Hearing people's unkind words, he grew angry with his mother's hunger.

Even Ajit, born from the womb of the younger queen, began to believe what people said—his mother had the hunger of a demon!

No one went near the demon queen anymore. Ajit said to his brother, "Let's run away together! Mother is insatiable; what if she goes for your blood next?"

The queen was angry because her child, too, had turned against her! She was furious!

The people, too, would not stop their whispers. *Women aren't supposed to have that kind of anger! The king had his flaws, too. He always got angry at his subjects' disobedience. But he was a man!*

That night, the queen's friends were invited to the palace.

Ajit told them, "We do not attend such demonic parties."

"Gosh! What terrible beasts!" said Kusum.

The queen was incensed at the treatment of her guests. Her friends, too, flew into a rage. They told Kusum,

"*Look at the boy, whole like the moon,*
He will become just a sphere soon!"

Immediately, Kusum became a round globe, bouncing around the palace floor.

The king was helpless without his elder son—he became completely mute and was too scared to act.

The only one left to stand up against his mother was Ajit. He rushed forward, sword in hand.

The queen cried out in a rage,

"*Look at you, iron-boy,*
Let's see you become an iron toy!"

Ajit became an iron globe and bounced and hit the golden globe.

The queen went up to the roof with the globes. It was choc-a-bloc with her people—family and friends of all kinds. People called them demons and demonesses, but who were they? They were the ones who loved food, those who messed with the king's laws, of course!

They all said,

"*We eat people, they all claim,*
How do we bear this loss of name?
Let's return from whence we came!"

The queen said,

"*I will not go from here,*
You lot go, far or near."

Saying this, the queen sent them to her native land—where her mother lived.

Then, the queen went to the bamboo forest by the river. There, she buried the gold and iron globes deep inside the earth. Her chest was heavy; her heart was full. The children remained captive.

The night passed.

2

Chaos ran unchecked in the kingdom on the following day.

The king had turned into a statue.

The princes were missing,

"That demoness must have eaten up the princes, too!" The people said.

They were ready to flee the kingdom—how could they live under a demon's rule?

On the other hand, the bamboo forest by the river swayed gently in the breeze. A farmer had gone there to cut down some trees. While doing so, he saw two eggs inside the bamboo.

"Could these be snake eggs?" he wondered.

The farmer picked them up and tossed them away. Instantly, the red and blue eggs cracked, and two princes—one red and one blue—came out. With crowns gleaming on their heads and swords clutched in their hands, they started running—who knows where to? The two princes, Kusum and Ajit, had been born again. They were now Prince Red Lotus and Prince Blue Lotus.

The farmer fainted in fear.

After some time, he regained consciousness. What was that he saw? The shell of the red egg was gold, and the shell of the blue egg was iron! He made a sickle from the iron shell and took the gold one home for his wife.

3

Where were Prince Red Lotus and Prince Blue Lotus going, sword in hand? To the land of the demons and beasts. They would only rest after they had defeated them all. But where was this land? Ajit, now Prince Blue Lotus, knew it very well—it was his mother's homeland, after all!

On their way, the two brothers reached the shade of a massive Ashwath tree, which housed the nest of the Byangoma and Byangomi birds. People across the land know these strange birds, which can fly just like other birds but are extraordinarily sharp of mind. Their intelligence is just like humans, if not even sharper. They talk just like humans, too.

Byangoma and Byangomi had just given birth to blind chicks. Byangomi was devastated. She was saying to Byangoma,

"*Who so kind might be,*

Would shed a few drops of blood,
So that my babies could see?"

Prince Red Lotus and Prince Blue Lotus heard her and said, "Who speaks from the treetop? We can give our blood."

Byangoma-Byangomi flew down. They looked so strange that the princes were speechless. Nevertheless, they slit their wrists and gave a few drops of blood.

The baby birds gained sight when a couple of drops of human blood fell upon their eyes. Byangomi cried, "Who are you princes who helped our children see?"

"Prince Red Lotus and Prince Blue Lotus," the princes said.

Byagoma asked, "Tell us what we can do for you."

"Can you take us to the land of demons and beasts?" Prince Blue Lotus asked.

"Of course! Climb onto our backs; we will fly you there."

Byangoma-Byangomi began the journey over mountains, rivers, jungles, and seas with the red and blue princes on their backs. Their babies flew behind them.

For seven days and six nights, they flew and flew. Then, the magical birds landed on a mountaintop on the seventh night. They said that the dark and unreachable valley belonged to the demons. Prince Blue Lotus's heart raced. He was related to this country by blood! It was his maternal family's land, after all.

Prince Blue Lotus was bright. He took a handful of *kalai* pulses from the basket and said to his brother, "Be careful! You will have to undergo various tests. Take this. If you are told to chew iron beans, chew these." Then he ventured into the pitch dark.

Smelling humans in the air, the demons and beasts came roaring. Prince Blue Lotus screamed,

"Call Aima. I am Ajit. I come from the land of men."

The demons stopped in their tracks. Aima was the oldest lady in their country. She came tottering on her sticks, huffing and panting, took Prince Blue Lotus in her arms, and cried out, "Oh my Bluey, oh my Ajit, oh my grand baby boy!"

A wave of happiness broke out. The demons began to dance. And from their throats came loud, tuneless songs!

No one noticed Prince Red Lotus, who stood there.

Then, when they finally stopped, exhausted, Aima sniffed the air and said, "But why do I smell human smell still?"

Then, everyone's eyes fell on Prince Red Lotus.

Prince Red Lotus trembled with fear. Prince Blue Lotus said, "Oh, silly you, Aima. Don't you know my brother?"

Neither Aima nor the demons could see well in the dark. Aima said, "If that's my grandson, let him chew the iron beans." She took a handful of it and handed it to Prince Red Lotus.

Prince Red Lotus quietly swapped the iron beans for the pulses, stuffed them in his mouth, and started chewing hard. The old woman was convinced that this was the grandson and was overcome with joy. In place of one, she now had two bright grandsons. She sat them on her lap and patted their heads—what love, what love!

They were well cared for in what others called the Palace of the Demons. The biggest event there was the feast. Everyone in that country was always ravenous! Everyone was full of life and ate heartily. Even the girls could enjoy all the sweets, fish, and meat, and no one bothered them or called them monsters, falling from their girly grace! Prince Red Lotus-Prince Blue Lotus had never seen such a sight before. No one was picky about what to eat! Red and Blue felt repulsed. They were witnessing real-life examples of a "monstrous appetite."

Then, they were offered a beautiful bed in an airy room to rest. But Prince Red Lotus-Prince Blue Lotus did not sleep. They plotted how to defeat the clan of demons in a fight!

5

Some younger demons and beasts were still somewhat suspicious about Prince Red Lotus. They sniffed the human smell from him. You might think that only humans are scared of demons. That's not true; demons are equally afraid, too! They, too, thought, "These humans are so strange! So picky about everything. All they do is turn up their noses or turn away their faces! They're not like us at all!"

The demons headed to check on Prince Red Lotus. They said, "If that boy is a human, I will cut his neck! Do you think only your race can show disgust? We'll show you!"

But the two princes were already up! They perked up at the sound of conversation and footsteps outside the door. Prince Blue Lotus said, "Shh, brother, just watch."

"Who is awake?" say the demon-beasts from outside the door.

Prince Blue Lotus says, "Before Prince Red Lotus, Prince Blue Lotus is awake."

No one could touch his brother without killing him first.

Prince Red Lotus also said, "Before Prince Blue Lotus, Prince Red Lotus is awake."

The chief of the beasts said, "Where are you, Prince Red Lotus? Where are you? If you are of demon or beast lineage, please spit and show us!"

Prince Blue Lotus immediately dropped two drops of hot ghee from the nearby lamp through the gap in the door. The stupid demons and beasts thought, "Wow! Even his spit is like a ball of fire; he must be the most demon-like demon of them all!"

The demon chief was still not convinced. He said, "Now show me your tongue."

So, Prince Blue Lotus poked his sword through the door's gap. The demon chieftain's finger was cut off when he touched the sword. He said, "Oh dear, oh dear! What a sharp tongue! I've never seen a demon so terrible!"

The test was over. The demons and beasts ran away. Prince Red Lotus and Prince Blue Lotus thought the demons could not see well in the dark and were not very intelligent. It wouldn't take long to kill them!

6

Aima doted on Red and Blue, her grandbabies. They befriended her and won her trust quite easily. They learned the secrets behind the birth and death of the demon clan. To the south of the kingdom was a well. Underneath it was a golden casket. Inside the casket lived Jiyonkati and Moronkati, a couple of hornets. Within them, they held the life and death of the demons.

That was it! One quiet afternoon, Prince Red Lotus and Prince Blue Lotus went to the well. Prince Red stood with the rope in his hand while Blue climbed down into the depths of the well. He brought up the magic casket.

As soon as light and the air touched the he-hornet, the heads of the demons in the kingdom began to tingle.

Then he cried, "Please spare me!"

But one of his legs was sliced off by a blow from Prince Red Lotus's sword. He writhed in agony. The she-hornet said, "So cruel! So very cruel! Traitors! Is this how you repay your hosts?"

By then, the legs of all the demons and the beasts in the kingdom had fallen off, just like the he-hornet's. Aima was falling over, once toward the front and once toward the back, without her leg. Limping and hobbling, they all reached the well.

Their shrieks echoed across the mountains and reached the ears of Byangoma and Byangomi. Their babies had grown up a little by then. The parents and children quickly flew in the direction of the wailing demons.

Byangoma asked, "Why are they limping?"

Byangomi replied, "Alas! I think we have brought their death on our backs!"

They flew straight to the well in the south of the kingdom. Byangomi said, "Children of good men, what have you done? What have you done?"

The princes said, "Killed the demons. Slayed the beasts."

Byangoma said, "This is a shame! Does a guest ever kill their host after enjoying their hospitality?"

Prince Blue Lotus interrupted, "Why not? They are strange! Weird!"

Byangoma said, "We are, too."

Prince Red Lotus said, "A daughter of theirs has my mother's blood on her hands."

Byangoma said, "What rubbish! She died of tuberculosis."

Prince Blue Lotus said, "They eat a lot. They are insatiable. There is no hope for them."

Byangomi said, "Let them eat. It's not like they've tried to eat you! Rather, they have done nothing but care for you lovingly."

Blue said, "Mothers and grandmothers shouldn't eat that much."

Byangoma said, "So what? I eat a lot, too."

Red said, "Their anger is uncontrollable. They're always ready to fight."

Byangomi said, "Really? It looks like you two are the ones with uncontrollable rage, always eager to fight."

Red and Blue were stunned. They stopped in their tracks. Byangoma and Byangomi's babies said, "You opened our eyes and gave us sight? But it looks like your eyes have been tightly shut all this while."

The demons were rolling about on the ground, clutching their remaining legs. It looked like old Aima had only moments of life left. Tears in her eyes seemed to say, "Grandbabies, this was what you had planned all this time?"

The demons had tears in their eyes! They cried, too! The princes couldn't believe their eyes. Were people wrong about demons, then? Were their eyes deceiving them now, or had their minds been deceiving them for many years?

Being different did not mean being evil, then. They remembered their demoness mother. A fire had raged in her eyes as she had cursed them. Did the heat of anger evaporate her tears?

Prince Red Lotus and Prince Blue Lotus's eyes also welled up. Byangoma and Byagomi flapped their wings and clapped. They said,

"*Bloodshot eyes, eyes with tears.*

A new thought, a shift in gears."

The baby birds chirped, "Your eyes have opened today! The eyes of your mind."

With their newly opened eyes, Prince Red Lotus and Prince Blue Lotus saw that their demoness mother had also crossed the seven seas and traveled to her home country. She also had one single leg—it had been lost along with the hornets'! She had run back to her homeland, worried about her relatives. There was no more anger in her eyes. It had been replaced by pain.

Prince Red Lotus and Prince Blue Lotus were full of regret. Poor mother! Everyone in their kingdom would badmouth her. She must have been very lonely.

They asked Byangoma and Byangomi, "How can we get their feet back?"

Byangomi said, "Cut your hand at the she-hornet Moronkati's feet and shed a drop of blood on them. Then Jionkati will get his leg back, and the demons will get back theirs, too."

The princes then, as before, cut off their fingers and washed the she-hornet's feet with a drop of blood. Thus, the broken legs of the demons and beasts were healed. They could walk around.

The demon queen and her mother, old Aima, stood before Prince Red and Blue, leaning on each other's shoulders.

Price Red Lotus and Prince Blue Lotus said together, "We made a mistake. Please forgive us."

What could Aima say? She let out a deep sigh.

Their mother said, "I have made a mistake, too, my sons. My anger is truly uncontrollable. Please forgive me."

Prince Red Lotus said, "Let's go back, mother."

The demon queen said, "No, my son. I'd rather stay here, as a strange girl in a strange country. You return home. If you ever remember your mother and grandmother, and if you can drop your swords and love with all your hearts, come again."

Once again, Prince Red Lotus and Prince Blue Lotus sat on Byangoma-Byangomi's back again. They would return home.

Byangomi said, "This time, Prince Red Lotus and Prince Blue Lotus, you have truly woken up."

The two brothers nodded.

Prince Red Lotus said, "Before Prince Blue Lotus, Prince Red Lotus is awake."

"Before Prince Red Lotus, Prince Blue Lotus awake," whispered Prince Blue Lotus.

SOMETHING TO THINK ABOUT

Is everything strange always evil? Do we think of anything different from ourselves as terrible? Is it always as awful as we initially thought?

THE STORY OF THE STORY

The story of 'Lalkamal, Neelkamal' *is popular. Audio-recorded songs written accordingly also gained popularity in the radio era. It depicted the good and evil queen and two princes' spine-tingling expeditions.*

In this new story, the journey is intended to take place in the outside world and the characters' mental worlds so that the characters can recognize new truths. Byangoma and Byangomi have been their teacher.

The Golden Stick and the Silver Stick

1

The prince of Birnagar galloped across his kingdom, surveying the land with a sense of duty. But to tell you the truth, he knew in his head that he had to find himself a princess, too. All the better! If he bumped against some damsel in distress on his travels, he'd slay the demons, rescue her, swiftly put a garland around her neck, and marry her. That simple! In all the stories he's heard since his childhood, that was how the prince married the princess.

On and on, on and on, how many nights, how many days pass! The horse's legs no longer moved. The prince's throat dried. Suddenly, he arrived at a vast kingdom. "Ah! Finally," the prince exclaimed.

Entering the kingdom, he saw, just like in the stories of his childhood, with her body on a bed of gold and feet on a bed of silver, lying a princess! The prince called her many times. The princess did not get up. Then the prince saw a golden reed on the head of the princess and a silver reed on her feet.

The prince was delighted. This is precisely what he thought would happen! That is what is written in the books. The prince did what princes in fairy tales have done for ages. He took the stick from the head toward the feet and the stick from the feet toward the head.

Just as written in the books of old, opening her lotus-flower-like eyes, the princess sat up and said, "Who are you? God or the devil? Monster or human? How did you come to this land of demons? Run, run!

The prince's soul dried up hearing the word "demon." But still, he was a prince! What would people say if he ran away? And how would he win the princess? So, he said, "O princess, tell me first, why are you in this demon land?"

The maiden said, "This kingdom used to be my father's. My mother passed away a long time ago, and sometime later, my father followed her.

"When the king died, a demoness and her grandson, a demon prince, took control of the kingdom. They had a hundred brave demon warriors with them. My family ran away as soon as they saw this frightening army!

"I stayed back. I thought maybe this was a blessing in disguise. They will kill me, and I will be reunited with my parents again.

"But they didn't do that. The demoness took pity on me. She said she wanted to raise me. So, I started living with them. In the daytime, they go hunting, sometimes close by or far away. Before they go out, they turn the golden and silver sticks and put me to sleep. They come back at night, turn the sticks again, and wake me up."

The prince conquered his fear and said,

"*O princess dear, I am the son of the king,*
You must know the duties it brings.
I entered the open door to a damsel rescue,
Help me so that I may save poor you."

"Finally!" The princess thought. "Finally, someone like me—someone who looks like me and speaks the same language. I'm sure I can trust him."

At that moment, the kingdom began to tremble and shake with the footsteps of demons. Their cries could be heard, too.

"*Fee fie fo fum, a human smell, oh so yum!*
Let's put him in our tum, here we come, here we come!"

The princess said to the prince, "Swap the reeds and put me to sleep. Then, run to the temple and hide under the flowers and leaves!"

The prince did as he was told.

2

On the other hand, the old demoness arrived with her grandson, chanting, "Fee fie fo fum."

She said,

"*A human smell, a human smell!*
My nose knows the scent so well,

Once I get my hands on him,
I'll snap his neck and have my din.'
Speak up, girl, where is he, do tell!'

The princess looked at them innocently and said, "I'm the only human here. Eat me if it pleases you."

The old demoness replied, "Oh, my dear granddaughter, how can I do that? I love you so much. I have so many dreams—I will get you married to my grandson!"

The demon-grandson stood shyly. He was burly and big with a massive mop of curly hair, a thick mustache, and a shy smile at the corner of his mouth.

The princess said with playful anger, "You all are suspicious of me too often! It's because I'm not of your kind."

The demon prince said, "Oh maiden, why are you angry? Who dares to eat you? Just see how much food we've brought for you."

Saying this, he took out a bunch of grapes and bananas from a basket to cool the princess's anger.

The princess ate, gave her arms a good stretch, and went to cook rich, spicy curries for the demons. The preparations were grand! The demons came daily and gave the princess the spoils of their hunt. She cooked for them, served them, and watched them eat. Then, she picked up the lice jumping around the grandma demon's hair and crushed them against a stone. Afterward, the demons went to sleep. The next day, they prepared to hunt again while the princess rested. Rather, she was forced to sleep—the sleep of the golden and silver sticks.

The next day, the moment the footsteps of the demons faded away, the handsome prince came out from behind the flowers and leaves of the temple. He woke the princess up by exchanging the golden and silver sticks. The two met. The prince said,

"How can it go on like this? What is the way to slay a demon?"

"Why? Don't you know how to fight in a battle?" the princess asked.

"Ah, that is not so," said the prince. "Demons are mighty. We can't just fight with them and win. They are the masters of their lives. You haven't read any stories, it seems."

"Then?" Asked the princess.

The prince said, "You must find the hidden key to their lives. Those rascals hide the key to their lives in butterflies, hornets, birds—and many more creatures! Maybe in a river, under a lake, or deep in a well! It's tough to find. Your task is to soothe them, pat them on the head, and find out the whereabouts of this key. Then, I will kill that insect or bird, and the game ends. It's much easier than killing demons with swords."

The princess opened her eyes wide and said, "Really? It goes like this?"

The prince said, "Of course. That's right."

The princess said, "Then?"

The prince said, "Then I will marry you. I will take you to my country. When I become the king, you will be the queen. Then you can sleep comfortably in the seven-story palace."

The princess said, "What about my kingdom?

"Well, that will become a district of my kingdom, of course. I will place one of my favorite generals here. He will rule."

The princess said, "I want to get my kingdom back. Otherwise, I will not give you the secret of the demons' lives."

The prince burst out laughing. He said, "This is why education is essential! It's a shame you spent so many days sleeping. A kingdom never belongs to its princess. The kingdom belonged to your father. It should go to your brother next. But you don't have one, so it goes to your husband-to-be, that means me!"

The princess stared in disbelief. She had been away from the world and its ways for a long time. Her days were spent sleeping. Her nights were spent cooking and feeding.

After persuading the princess, the prince put her to sleep again. Then he went back to the temple and hid.

3

When the demons returned that day and woke the princess, she showered them with much affection and care. She made a buffet of all their favorite foods—a mule head in a stew, lizard tails in a chutney–sweet and tangy that when the grandma finished eating, burped contentedly, and sat with her legs spread out, the princess asked, "Oh, Aima! You must be so tired after hunting across so many distant lands! Come, let me pluck your gray hairs for you." The princess gently ran her fingers through the old demoness's hair.

The old grandmother said, "Yes, my grandbaby. My two legs are tired and aching. Will you massage them with some oil?"

The maiden said, "Of course!"

She began to massage her legs and started to sniff her nose repeatedly.

The old woman asked, "Oh dear, do you have a cold?"

The princess said, "No, Aima. I weep with grief."

The old woman said, "Oh no! What for?"

Then the maiden spoke, "Aima, you are old. If you die, the demons will eat me!"

Aima said, "Oh, silly!! The key of Aima's life and death is in Aima's hand. I won't die unless I wish to myself."

"Where is this key?" asked the maiden.

The old woman was old. She had the wisdom of experience. She said,

"Wait, let me get you married first. Let me make you my granddaughter-in-law. I will tell you then."

After saying this, the old woman went to sleep. The princess saw that there was great danger ahead of her! How would the secret of the life-death key be recovered?

The old woman's grandson, the demon prince, was walking past to the bedroom. He gave off a strong smell of sweat. Who knew how many lice were in his shaggy hair? The princess didn't like him at all. Most of all, she disliked his mustache. But the demon prince was crazy about the princess!

He hides his feelings,

His love and longing.

He's a prince but would gladly be her slave,

The princess is the one thing that he badly craves.

At first, the princess was very afraid of him. But she doesn't feel scared any longer. Rather, seeing the shyness of such a big man makes her laugh.

The princess got an idea upon seeing the demon prince. She clutched onto him and asked, "Why do you get so shy when you see me?"

The demon prince felt as if all of his dreams were coming true. He began to stutter.

The princess said, "I would be devastated if someone were to kill you."

Tears of happiness welled in the demon prince's eyes.

The princess said, "If you trust me, please tell me where the secret key to your life is hidden. Only if I know for myself will I feel reassured."

The demon prince hesitated for just a moment. Something glittered at the corner of his eye. Then he gently whispered into the princess's ear,

"A crystal pillar in the lake,
There lives a seven-hooded snake.
A wound within the serpent's head,
The only way to make demons dead."

ꟷ

The demon prince went off to sleep. But the princess tossed and turned the whole night, thinking of what to do next. She did not know why she felt sad. She kept wondering about what had glittered in the corner of the demon prince's eye. Was it a tear? Had he caught on to her plan, then?

But if he was on to her, why would he reveal the secret of his death?

He had confided in her with so much trust and revealed the biggest secret of his life. Wouldn't she be sinning if she broke his trust? But so what if it was? He was a gigantic, lice-headed demon, after all!

Why should she bother herself with such unpleasant thoughts? She had golden days ahead of her—a seven-story palace, the title of queen, she'd never have to cook again, and she could sleep restfully.

But would that sleep really be different from her sleep now? True, she lived a life of labor—she had to cook for and serve a clan of demons. But the life of a queen didn't allow much independence either. Was it just another side of the same coin?

Was it necessary to take the lives of the demons? Especially after they had bestowed so much trust on her . . . Would tampering with that bond of trust be an act of bravery?

But . . . the demons had taken over her father's kingdom. She had to take back control. But what if power transferred from the demon's hands to those of the prince? Where would that leave her?

She'd be the same porcelain doll,
Trapped between sticks of silver and gold,
Life of leisure and idleness would pass,
And lo! One day, she'd be old.

The princess paced up and down, her thoughts chasing one another. The moon had already set, and the eastern sky was turning red. The demons gradually stopped snoring.

They didn't know that danger lay ahead. Perhaps one of them sensed it . . . although was he certain? The princess was confused.

After exchanging the sticks and putting the princess to sleep, the demon grandmother took her grandson and her army and went out for their daily hunt.

5

The prince anticipated this opportunity. He shook off the flowers and leaves from his body and woke the princess from her sleep.

Eagerly, he asked, "What did they say? Did you find out the secret?"

The princess replied, "Yes, I did. But my conscience is holding me back. I can't reveal it."

The prince was shocked. He couldn't make head or tail of her words. He had never read of this in the fairy tales.

He asked, "Your what? What is holding you back? What do you mean?"

"Trust," the princess said, "breaking it is a sin."

The prince's rage held no bounds,

"Idiot!" he screamed, his voice echoing around.

His shot at bravery was slipping away,

The stupid girl had drowned him near the shore of the bay.

All his pleas, all his entreaties were in vain. A necklace of seven strands, a golden palace, new and grand—no bribe changed the princess's mind.

"Fine!" The prince then said in a fit.

"Rot and die here then, so be it!"

The prince put the princess back to sleep and galloped away from the kingdom as fast as possible. He had to find a princess who wanted to be saved.

That night, the demons returned and woke the princess. They ate and drank like they did every day. When it was late at night, and everyone was fast asleep, the demon prince came to the princess. "Why didn't you give him the key to our lives?" he asked.

"You knew all along?" the princess asked.

"Everyone knew," the demon prince said. "It's written in the books. It's the way the world works, after all. The princess learns the secret of the demons' lives and tells her sweetheart."

"I couldn't do it!" the princess cried. "It would have been deception!"

The two sat in silence for a long time. When it was almost dawn, the demon princess said to the princess, "It was wrong of us to keep you imprisoned here. We, too, have sinned."

The princess replied, "What is a sin, what is a virtue, which is a good deed, and which is a bad one? It's not always possible to learn the meaning of these by reading the stories of old. It takes time to realize their true meaning. Even if your realization has dawned late, it's good that it has come."

The demon prince said, "You don't want to remain a prisoner here. You don't want the prince either. This is very strange! What is it that you want?"

"I don't know what I want just now. It will take me time to understand, but I know what I don't want," the princess replied.

"*When the world is turning,*
When the birds are flying,
When sea waves are dancing,
When flowers are blooming,
I don't want to remain asleep.
Everything I want to see, everything!
I want to smell,
I want to taste,
I want to feel."

"So be it!" said the demon prince.

The old demoness woke up right on time the following day. When she came to put the princess to sleep, what did she see? The golden bed was empty, and so was the silver bed. The first rays of the sun glimmered on the golden stick and the silver stick lying on the empty bed.

SOMETHING TO THINK ABOUT

Be it "Prince Red Lotus, Prince Blue Lotus" or this story, we see in various stories that the prince kills the demons without defeating them in battle but by taking advantage of their trust and seizing the key to their lives. Isn't that deception?

THE STORY OF THE STORY

In the original story, the prince exchanges the golden and silver sticks to awaken the princess. She then manipulates and deceives the demons into revealing the whereabouts of their life force. The prince kills the moth that holds within it the key to the demons' lives and destroys their entire clan. He then marries the princess and returns to his kingdom.

In the new story, the princess questions her traditional role—that of a betrayer pretending to be someone virtuous and good.

The Scholar Fox

1

There once was a fox who wished to become a great scholar. He sat down in the forest to give lessons to a wide audience whom he had roped into becoming his students—an audience of beetles, grasshoppers, turtles, frogs, earthworms, cockroaches, and many more.

He was full of pomp and air. He swung his cane more often than he spared his wisdom for the pupils. What a learned creature!! But in reality, he knew almost nothing. He had stolen Master Dada's old, discarded spectacles and taken them with him to the city after he was severely beaten up. He had stolen some heavy, impressive-looking books and taken them too. Those books were no longer helpful to anyone, so they were thrown away. The name of those books were *Telephone Directory*. The fox memorized all the names he found there. Then he went to his classroom, broken spectacles on his nose, and loudly began,

"*Chotto, khotto, motto*
Upadhyay notto
Bones do the khiski
Stakidim Dimisky."

The critters and crawlers were mighty impressed.

An alligator heard his teachings and said, "The insects and spiders have learned so much from this great creature! Why should my girls stay away from his teachings and remain stupid?"

Gator-mum said, "I don't know. I have my misgivings about him."

But Alli-dad said, "Things have changed. We won't get good sons-in-law if we don't educate our girls."

The Alli-girls asked, "Why don't we attend a government school?

We'll read, we'll write.
And have a future so bright.
Learning new things,
What opportunities will it bring?"

The Alli-dad paid no attention to them. Why did they need to learn so much? They only needed enough education to secure husbands . . .

He appeared in the Scholar Fox's classroom with his seven Alli-girls. The fox saw seven juicy, young, innocent girls before him. He told their father,

"*So simple, so charming!*
Just like the Goddess of Learning
They will become in just a week!
The kind of husband that they seek
You will find readily, I promise thee.
Return in seven days, and for yourself, see!"

With much fanfare, the Alli-girls were taught to put chalk to slate for the first time that day, and the Alli-dad returned home happily.

Then?

The teacher chose one Gator-baby every day. He sat her down on his lap and lovingly taught her,

"*Chotto, khotto, motto*
Upadhyay notto
Bones do the khiski
Stakidim Dimisky."

The Alli-girls felt light-headed. They wanted to vomit. Bile seemed to run through their veins. The fox picked up his student of the day and gulped her down with water.

The Alli-girls noticed that one of their sisters disappeared every day. She didn't return, so they cried, "Mother, help us! Father, save us!"

But their thin voices got lost in the distant, vast forest. They had nothing to do but beat their heads in despair.

2

Six days passed. The Alli-dad thought, "Tomorrow, my scholar daughters will return." He told his wife, "Listen, fry up some hilsa-skins—our second daughter loves them! And some tangy *Bowal* fish stew for the fifth one!" The Alli-dad issued a few more commands, then wore his old jute shawl and wrapped his fraying net around him. He wore an overturned dinghy on his head like a turban as he set out to bring home his daughters; his father's heart could hardly wait to see them!

"Mr. Scholar, let me see my daughters and how wise they have become!"

The fox quickly exited the tunnel and said, "Please come, please sit down! Beetles, where are you? Fan him! I will call the crocodile beauties one by one."

Saying this, he went into the hole and grabbed the remaining Gator baby's neck. He gritted his teeth and said to her, "Beware! Don't you dare tell the truth to your father! You know what happens if you tell the truth? You'll be shunned in society. No one will marry you."

The lone Gator baby was cowering in fear. She nodded silently. "This is number one," said the fox, holding her up from the hole. The hatchling saw her father!

The fox then brought her down to the ground. "Number two," he said with a twinkle in his eye.

"How stupid father is!" The Gator baby thought. "He did not understand what was suitable for his girls! All six of my sisters died!"

Meanwhile . . .

"Number three."

"Number four."

The Gator baby thought, "Even if society discards us, will we die? Is being married more important than being alive? What if I scream but still don't survive?"

"Number five."

"I think I'm going to die. But I have to speak up. No other father should hand over his child to such a monster."

The moment the fox said, "Number six . . ."

The Alli-girl raised her voice, gathered all her strength, and shouted faintly, "Father! Help! He will eat me!"

Immediately, the fox left the den. His teeth were shining, his tongue was watering, his eyes were wide, and his body was shaking. But then the father crocodile jumped into the hole. The fox forgot everything else and fled! He broke through the forest and started running.

The Alli-dad saw the bones of his children scattered all around. The blood had dried on the ground. How much he slapped his forehead with his tail!

He cried inconsolably! But by that time, the fox was already far away. Alli-dad returned home with futile anger and only one daughter.

3

As the fox scholar ran and ran, he came upon a field of brinjals. His stomach was writhing in hunger, so he happily ate some brinjal without knowing who it belonged to. All of a sudden, a small thorn pricked his nose. No matter how much he sneezed or blew his nose, the thorn did not come out. Finally, the fox went to a barber's house.

The barber was very kind. A good man. How tragically, the fox was crying! The barber's heart melted by his tears. He said, "Ah ha! You must have got caught somewhere badly! You're in big trouble! Wait, let me bring my clippers. I'll get the thorn out."

But who can escape their karma?

The barber accidentally,
Sliced the fox's nose off.
With a thorn, a nose cut for free!

The fox cried and said, "Oh! No! Look what you've done! Sliced away my nose! Piece it back together; otherwise, I will complain to the king."

The good man said, "Sorry, brother! Forgive me, or else I'll be dead."

"First, give your clippers as compensation," said the fox.

Blessed with a clipper instead of a nose, the noseless fox scholar set off once again. Along the way, he saw a potter sitting with his wares. The fox was bored with the clippers; he now wanted the pots. What did he do? He secretly threw stones and broke his clippers. Then he told the potter, "Let's see how your pot is; hold my clippers while I check it out."

When the potter took the clippers, the fox said, "There! You broke it, didn't you? My favorite pair! I am going to complain to the king."

The potter was not an intelligent man. He said, "Sorry, brother! I beg you, forgive me, or else I'll be dead."

The fox said, "Then give me a pot as compensation."

The potter handed over a pot with a sigh of relief. The fox started walking again with the pot.

On the other side of the road, a bridegroom was returning home with his newlywed bride. The procession was bursting firecrackers and fireworks. The bride dressed in red could be seen through the gaps of the palanquin.

The fox thought, "Lovely girl! I will get married, too. I want this girl to be my wife."

Saying this to himself, he deliberately placed the pot in their path. If someone accidentally broke it, he would seek compensation. But what happened next exceeded the fox's expectations. A cracker came out of nowhere and fell into the pot. The pot burst. What else could happen next? The fox came out of the bush, rolling his eyes and puffing his neck. He said, "Do you think you can do whatever you want and get away with it just because you got married? Lighting fireworks in the middle of the road! Didn't you get any other place? If you know what's good for you, mend my broken pot. Otherwise, I am going to complain to the king."

The bridegroom was at sea. The whole procession said, "We're sorry, brother. We beg your forgiveness. If you don't forgive us, we will die."

"Give me the bride instead of my pot," said the fox.

What else could the poor groom do? He had heard in a movie somewhere, "*If your wife goes, then you're without a wife, but if you go to jail, then you're without a life!*" The groom gave the bride to the fox and ran away with his friends and relatives.

After getting the bride, the fox can hardly hold back his excitement. The bride is veiled. The fox thinks, "I have a shy girl, as sweet as honey. She'll massage my hands and feet. Cook for me and feed me. Time for domestic life!"

Meanwhile, the girl behind the veil was seething with anger. She was not a naïve alligator hatchling! She was a human girl with ample knowledge of good and evil, of what to value and what to discard. She knew very well how to bring such foxes to their knees; she was just waiting for the right time. And she thought bitterly about her parents' choice—how could they have married her off to a man like this? It was good that she was rid of him. A groom who does not value his wife should die!

The fox appeared in the house of a priest with his bride. The priest's wife was sitting in the yard cutting vegetables. The bride sat quietly beside her as if butter wouldn't melt in her mouth.

The fox said, "Greetings, Mrs. Priest! I wish to marry. This is my bride. Call Mr. Priest out."

The priest's wife went into the house to call the priest. What did the bride do? With one swift stroke of the priest's wife's knife, she chopped off the fox's head, sending it rolling across the floor.

But the lips of the cut head still talked! They said,

"*Six girls, so beautiful*
I ate once with glee
Perhaps that's why,
My sin has returned to eat me!"

Then his lips stopped moving.

His eyes did not open.

The priest's wife cried out.

The priest cursed the bride.

The bride could not care less. She removed her veil. Neither did she look exquisite nor was she ugly. Her hair was askew, and the sandalwood on her forehead had smudged. But there was something about her eyes—so bright, as if she had much more to do.

The girl walked away quietly, right before the eyes of the priest and his wife.

SOMETHING TO THINK ABOUT

You know what happens if you tell the truth? Society shuns you. No one marries you! Why is this?

THE STORY OF THE STORY

The original story is about a cunning fox who eats a crocodile's seven sons (not daughters) and then deceives many people. The bride is a secondary character; the fox wants to marry her, but the poor bride suddenly dies. In this version, we see the fox punished at the hands of the bride.

Shukhu and Dukhu

There was once a weaver who had two wives. The two wives had a daughter each. Of course, the two wives were constantly bickering and clashing with each other. The one who could put up a show of greater strength would win that battle. The weaver sat cursing his luck. "What a bad idea!" he thought. "No one should have two wives in one lifetime . . ."

At first, the weaver had only one wife, but the moment she gave birth to a daughter, he brought home a second wife, hoping for a son. The elder wife and her daughter, Shukhu the joyous one, were filled with malice. The new bride got an earful when she stepped into her new home. On top of that, within a year, she, too, gave birth to a daughter. Her daughter was named Dukhu, the woeful one. The elder wife and Shukhu could barely hold in their laughter. "Hah! How about that!"

The weaver soon died, lamenting the absence of a son. After his death, fights broke out once again over who would inherit the tiny house and his meager savings. Finally, the dead weaver's belongings were divided between the two wives, who then parted ways.

Despite her widowhood, Shukhu's mother, who was fond of a leisurely life, enjoyed rich food and indulged in luxuries like shrimp curry and fish heads. Her behavior shocked the village, who praised Dukhu's mother for her modesty. They said, "Just go and see what a good widow Dukhu's mother is! She weaves *gamchha* cloth and sells it and she survives only on vegetable broths and rice. She's raised her girl so well. She's happy with the little that she has. And look at Shukhu's mother, off raising a little princess, isn't she?"

Both wives now had to spin cotton themselves, laying it out to dry in the sun. Shukhu and Dukhu were tasked with watching over the cotton and thread. As they spent their days together, the animosity between the girls faded. They began talking secretly behind their mothers' backs.

Dukhu said, "Sister, you are very outspoken. You quarrel too much."

Shukhu said, "You, little sister, are too quiet for your good. You won't protest even if someone slaps you seven times. You'd just sit there and cry!"

Dukhu said, "That's true, I'm not brave like you. But it doesn't need to become a woman to be so brave."

Shukhu said, "You get scared too easily, sister. Living in fear is like living in death."

One day, as the two girls watched over the cotton and thread, a gust of wind blew it away. Dukhu started crying in fear of what her mother would say. Shukhu said, "There's no point in crying. Let's follow the wind. It's bound to return our cotton!"

At that moment, the two sisters noticed both mothers had come to the fence after finishing their baths. One of the mothers exclaimed, "What incredible luck! We've received a summons from the Old Mother. If we manage to please her, she won't just return the cotton and thread we lost—she might even reward us with gold, diamonds, and perhaps, if she's in a particularly good mood, find us a princely bridegroom. Hurry, hurry!"

Shukhu's mother said, "Run faster than Dukhu, Shukhu."

Dukhu's mother said, "Run faster than Shukhu, Dukhu."

Shukhu and Dukhu kept running after hearing their mothers. The mothers slowly faded behind.

As they went, they saw a cow tied on the side of the road. She said, "Where are you going? Please clean my shed before you go."

Shukhu said, "Oh no! The cotton floats away."

Dukhu said, "Yet, we should listen to what she says . . ."

Then, the two made a decision. Dukhu cleared the dung around the cow and Shukhu gave her hay to eat and water to drink. "Dear lady cow, adieu," the two said. "Our cotton flies away. We will stop by you and clean your shed again on our way back." The cow happily agreed and gave them a pail full of milk.

Shukhu and Dukhu resumed their journey. A little down the path, a banana plant called, "Where are you two going? Here I am, all tangled up in weeds and creepers. Clear them for me, please. Look how the bananas are drooping down. Pick them up."

Dukhu was always willing to listen to others, but Shukhu insisted that the cotton would float away. Once again, they made a pact. They sheared away the weeds and creepers from the banana plant and said, "Let someone else pick the bananas, or we'll do it ourselves, but on our way back. Our cotton is floating away!"

The banana plant was happy and gave them a bunch of bananas. Shukhu and Dukhu ate the bananas, drank the milk, and set off again.

A moss-covered tree a little far ahead called out too.

"Wait, wait! Could you two please clear the rubbish around my trunk? Gather all the leaves and other waste and burn them in a fire."

Shukhu and Dukhu discussed the situation.

The poor tree must be feeling itchy with so much junk near its trunk. They decided that they would sweep away all the debris, and later in the day, they'd gather the leaves and light a fire. After they were done, the moss-covered tree happily gifted them a vase full of coins.

A little further down, they were stopped yet again by a horse. "Will you give me a few blades of grass on your way, please?" it asked. Dukhu and Shukhu had now started thinking the same way. They did not have a dispute this time. They each cut some grass and gave it to the horse. The horse gave them the tiny foal of a winged horse. The little horse flapped its wings and flew them away.

After some time, the sisters arrived in front of a spotless white house. An old lady sat at a spinning wheel in one corner of the courtyard. Threads were being woven together in a fraction of a second, and entire sarees were being made in the blink of an eye! Dukhu and Shukhu were the daughters of a weaver, yet they had never seen such quick and intricate work before. They stood gaping in amazement. A gentle breeze whispered in their ears that this woman was none other than the old lady on the moon—the one who sat there, spinning at her wheel all night and day!

"Is she not married?" Dukhu asked. "Does she have no one?"

Shukhu said, "Someone who can spin so skillfully and weave so beautifully is the queen of queens themselves! Did our mothers marry and find great happiness? Ever since our father died, their fate has been to weave towels all day long."

The old lady smiled like moonlight, brushing her milk-foam hair. Two little girls, sweet as grains of sugar, had come to her door looking for cotton and thread—one naive and gullible, one sharp as a tack. The old woman was

greatly amused. She said, "Oh my moon-faced girls, come, come! There are towels in the next room. There is oil and soap, too. Clothes are kept there. Bathe yourselves and come. There is food in the other room. Eat well, and then I will give you your cotton and thread."

Dukhu was true to her nature: She took a rag-like towel, used just a pinch of oil on her head, and as little soap as possible, wore the coarsest saree she could find, and ate a simple meal of fermented rice.

Shukhu, too, was true to her nature: She took generous helpings of oil and soap, wiped herself with the nicest towel she could find, wore the finest saree, and sat down for a five-course meal. "All these lovely things are available for free; why shouldn't I enjoy them?" she thought.

The old lady was now well able to understand their characters. She laughed heartily. "Both of you need to learn a lesson," she said. "Dukhu, why do you opt for the poorest options even when better things are available?"

Dukhu said, "Mother has taught me to be content with little. Girls are not supposed to be greedy, she says."

The old woman said, "She's wrong. And Shukhu, just because a lot is available, do you have to take all of it? Don't you have any sense of proportion?"

Shukhu said, "Oh, but what if I never get the opportunity again?"

The old woman said, "You will get it for sure. If you deserve it, you will get it. Good work leads to good results, just as the spinning wheel spins to weave the thread!"

Then the two sisters said simultaneously, "You will teach us? Will you teach us? I want to cut thread like you! I want to weave sarees like you! I don't want anything else."

The old woman laughed and said, "Well, well! Did no one tell you what to ask for from me? Gold . . . jewels . . . husbands . . . did no one tell you?"

The two sisters said, "Make us the best of weavers. We will earn gold ourselves."

The old woman of the moon said, "That's right. The wealth that is found does not last, Shukhu. Wealth has to be earned. There is dignity in earning it. It lets one hold their head high, understand, Dukhu? One with her head high is a good girl, not a coward."

Dukhu and Shukhu said, "Right, right!"

The old woman said, "All the girls who came before did not understand my words. Do you know how you understood them?"

Dukhu and Shukhu said, "How?"

The old woman said, "In friendship and love. A girl with a little bit of Shukhu and a little bit of Dukhu is a winner. You two are friends, aren't you? That's why you learned the lesson so easily."

Dukhu and Shukhu hugged each other. Since then, Shukhu has learned to spin the wheel and Dukhu to weave the loom. They divided the vase's gold in half and sent it to the two mothers on the back of the winged horse. Along with it, they sent a letter.

"*We are doing well here.*
Spinning, looms, and threads galore.
Chandburi's life revolves around these.
Why should we need more?

Forget the quarrel, my dear mother,
Raise your head a little higher!
We're learning knitting and learning life.
Learning to be a human, not a wife,
Different than before, we will be,
You'll bless us so much, just wait and see!

This vase of coin is sent for you,
By your daughters, Shukhu and Dukhu."

SOMETHING TO THINK ABOUT

The girl with both Dukhu and Shukhu's qualities is the true winner. Why do you think so?

THE STORY OF THE STORY

Once again, it was a good girl versus a bad girl story. The evil girl is Shukhu, along with her mother, because they seek happiness. The good girl is Dukhu, with her mother, because they endure suffering. The "evil" gets severe punishment—a python snake eats Shukhu under the curse of the old lady of the moon, and her mother dies from a blow to her head. In contrast, Dukhu gets a beautiful prince as her groom.

Can the little girl and her mother, who wanted happiness, be considered evil just for that? So, we mixed up what is good and what is evil. We made Shukhu and Dukhu friends, thereby redefining the meaning of happiness.

The One and a Half Finger

1

Once there lived a woodcutter and his wife. I can't tell you how much the villagers abused them for not having children! The woodcutter's wife prayed so hard and kept, oh, just too many fasts! The woodcutter kept praying to Shasthi, the goddess of children and birth, "Mother, we are unfortunate. Please send someone to fill our laps!"

One night, the woodcutter's wife had a dream. In it, the goddess of birth and children, Mother Shasthi, revealed herself and said,

"*Wash with oil and vermillion with lots of joy,*

You will get a golden boy."

The wife got up at dawn, washed her head with oil, and smeared vermilion. The woodcutter had gone to the forest to cut wood. Beside the gurgling fountain, an old woman gave a cucumber to the woodcutter and said, "Give this to your wife. She must eat the whole thing—throwing away nothing. Then your house will light up with a baby boy."

The woodcutter was thrilled. Dropping the wood, he ran home. He told his wife everything but forgot to add the instruction that "the whole cucumber had to be eaten, not a bit to be thrown away." His wife also went to the kitchen, threw away the ends of the cucumber, and ate the remaining part. While eating lunch at noon, the woodcutter noticed the cucumber ends thrown away on one side of the courtyard.

"Oh no! Alas!" The woodcutter said. "Woman, you threw away the ends!"

By then, crows were pecking at the discarded cucumber ends. The woodcutter's wife couldn't eat them anymore. The woodcutter threw away his plate of rice and went into the house all furious!

2

What else? Even after so many rituals and fasting, finally, a girl was born. No one gives a hoot when a girl is born; the conch is not blown. Poor people's homes are even darker. When a girl is born, her parents spend sleepless nights worrying about her marriage from the moment of her birth.

On top of that, the girl born to the woodcutter was even more difficult to marry! She was shorter than one could imagine, tinier than the tiniest! She was just about one and a half fingers tall.

Angry at his wife, the woodcutter left home. His wife cried. She fended for herself by collecting and foraging for wood. Their daughter grew up but did not grow. Who cared about her? Her mother once went to the river, intending to jump into it. But when she looked at her daughter's face, she couldn't go through with it.

Slowly, the girl stood up and began to talk. Wiping her mother's tears, she said, "I am leaving to bring my father back."

3

But where was he? Where had he gone? The one-and-a-half-finger girl began to move, looking for her father. Ants came at her, and so did the grasshoppers, but she was fearless. "Move, you creepers!" She commanded, dismissing them. At last, dancing and walking, the girl reached the king's house. She saw a poor woodcutter cutting wood under the blazing sun.

The one-and-a-half-finger girl realized this was her father. She said, "Father, why did you leave me? Come home! Mother cries so much!"

The woodcutter was surprised—his daughter! So what if her father had forgotten her? She had not forgotten him! The woodcutter realized his mistake, but he had no way to return. He said, "The king has bought me with money. What do I do?"

The one-and-a-half-finger girl went to the king.

"Your majesty, please return my father to me. He has cut a lot of wood. He has worked off his price."

The king was ruthless. He had bought this woodcutter as a slave from the market—how could he let him leave?

"Repay his cost, daughter
Then only will I leave your father."

The one-and-a-half-finger girl realized that the world ran on money. She left to fetch money and free her father.

She went into the forest. Suddenly, she felt a pull at her hair. Behind her was a golden frog.

The frog stood in her way and said,

"Hey, hey dearie,
Why in such a hurry?"

"Get out of the way," said the girl.

The frog said, "I am the frog prince. Don't show your anger at me."

The girl says, "Well, what am I supposed to do with this information?"

The frog said, "My wife is also a frog. My father rejected me because my wife is of a low caste. She is trapped in a gourd shell on that dead tree. My father's soldiers captured her with the help of a sparrow. Either rescue my wife and get her off the tree, or I will marry you. I see we're the same height. Where else will I get such a small wife?"

The girl said, "Nonsense! Why don't you just say you need my help?"

The frog said, "Aren't I ashamed to ask for help from a girl?"

The one-and-a-half-finger girl said, "My father is a woodcutter, but I don't have an axe!"

The frog said, "Across the forest is the blacksmith's house. He will give you an axe if you give him a coin."

The girl said, "Where can I get coins? I could not free my father because I had no coins."

However, the girl went to the blacksmith's house, fell at his feet, and begged him to make her a one-finger tall axe.

The blacksmith was very upset. She had no coin, so why give her an axe? The girl said, "I don't have a father; my mother is crying." We are a family of woodcutters. We cut wood, but we don't even have an axe. Save me. When the time comes, I will repay your loan with interest."

The blacksmith understood that the girl was poor like him. He took pity on her. He made her a tiny axe.

The one-and-a-half-finger girl left with tears in her eyes.

The frog saw the axe and said, "Well done!!"

The dead tree collapsed after the two hacked at it for seven days and seven nights. The frog's wife was recovered from the gourd's shell.

The golden frog said happily, "I have a coin. Go, buy back your father."

The frog's wife said, "The king's son, the prince, is blind. You can bring back his sight with my spit."

The one-and-a-half-finger girl walked to the king's house with all her acquired things.

4

The one-and-a-half-finger girl reached the king's house again, dismissing the creepies and crawlies in her way.

"Here is your coin, your highness,
Now, my father, you must release."

The king said,

"This coin here,
It adds nothing to my life.
Your father will go
If Lochan gets a wife."

The name of the king's younger son was Padmalochan. The king's demands were many. Even though his son was blind, the king wanted a noble bride. But which noble family would marry off their daughter to a blind boy? Only if he could find a blind princess would his son get a wife. But he hadn't been able to find such a girl. That burden of this search now fell on the shoulders of the one-and-a-half-finger girl.

Her legs could barely move, her mind could not think, and her limbs had slackened, but the girl kept walking. Where could she find such a princess? She met the golden frog once again on the way. He said, "In the land where seven thieves live, the big thief is the king of thieves. His daughter is blind."

The one-and-a-half-finger girl thus walked to the country of thieves with a proposal on behalf of Prince Padmalochan.

After walking for miles and miles and miles, the one-and-a-half-finger girl finally fell asleep exhausted, on a mound of termites. At that time, the seven thieves had gone out together to steal. Just as the youngest thief's foot landed on the girl's neck, she shrieked and struck a blow with her axe.

The youngest thief cried out loud, and all the thieves were surprised. Who struck out so angrily? Was it a ghost? They started to chant the god Ram's name for protection.

Meanwhile, the one-and-a-half-finger girl noticed the seven brothers with large *sindhkathis* in their hands. She realized that the blacksmith who had helped her also made these sticks that were used to break into houses. Was this then the kingdom of the seven thieves? If so, she had to find the eldest thief, the king! She had to speak to him about the proposal.

She shook her hands and waved her legs, desperately trying to attract the attention of the trembling thieves. Finally, she climbed onto a taro leaf from the taro forest near the termite mound and came in line with their eyesight.

"Hahahahahah!" "Hihihihihihi!" "Hohohohohoho!" They fell over each other, laughing at the sight. A girl—that too such a tiny one—out at night—and with an axe in her hand! What a strange sight!

They fell on each other laughing hard.

The one-and-a-half-finger girl straightforwardly proposed,

"The king's son will get a wife,
To the thief king's daughter, he'll be hitched for life.
A blind bride for a blind groom.
Coin and jewels to fill a room!"

The eldest thief thought that the proposal was a decent one. How did it matter if his blind girl stayed here or lived somewhere else? And he'd get coin and jewels—enough to fill a room!

The seven brothers set out to talk to the king. The one-and-a-half-finger girl led them, and the thief brothers followed behind.

The blacksmith's shop was on their way. However, just like a tiger never changes its stripes, stealing was a thief's second nature. Although they were going to their future in-law's house, they couldn't resist stopping by the blacksmith's to swipe some sindhkathis before resuming their journey.

The one-and-a-half-finger girl arrived at the king's court with the seven thieves. She pointed to the eldest and said, "Your Majesty, this is King Taskarkumar of the kingdom of Harmad. His daughter is blind. He will give her to your son in marriage if he gets a hundred coins."

"He may be a thief, but he's a king too!" the king thought. The king bought the blind princess for a hundred coins. Her relatives were all allowed to stay in the royal guest house. People were sent to fetch the blind princess from the kingdom of thieves.

The king told the one-and-a-half-finger girl, "Tomorrow is the prince's wedding. Stay for the wedding feast, and then you may take your father and leave."

5

But just like a tiger never changes its stripes, stealing is a thief's second nature. The moment night fell, their hands began to itch as the lust for the king's riches flashed through their minds. In the quiet of the night, they stole from their future in-law's house and ran off. And then, they even went to steal from the people's houses. The kingdom was a prosperous one—wealth galore. They became intoxicated from the thrill of stealing but were finally caught by the kingdom's night watchmen. But how would the watchmen recognize them or know that their daughter would be married to the king's son? The thief brothers were all sent to jail.

The king got up in the morning and rushed to free his in-laws. But the thieves had changed their minds. The eldest thief said, "My girl may be blind, but her thieving skills are good, Wedding her to this land—no, I am no longer in the mood!"

Saying this, they left that country and went back to their own state. How can a marriage take place if the two families don't align in taste? Marriage is hardly child's play!

Meanwhile, the one-and-a-half-finger girl was preparing to attend the prince's wedding. She went to the weaver's house, where the weaver sewed her a ghaghra with scraps of cloth left behind from the queen's royal clothes. The gardener strung flower garlands for her nose, ears, neck, hands, and feet. The village cat became for her a horse. She went to the feast on the cat's back.

But when she got there, what did she see? The kingdom was abuzz with distress—there was crying in the palace. The king sat quietly, his head in his hands. His son was not getting married, and the royal line would not continue.

The one-and-a-half-finger girl saw great danger ahead of her. She would not get her father back even after all the trouble she had gone through.

She lost all her patience. "Your Majesty," she said, "please do not take offense. My father left my mother, saying that his line would not continue. You agree to marry your son into a clan of thieves just because they are royalty, too! Is family name truly so important? You say your son must get married, even if he never finds love within it! Why? Because of this obsession with preserving lineage? Even the golden frog's father shuns him because his wife is from a poor family. What is family? Why is preserving its good name so important? Do I not understand because I didn't go to school?"

The king beat his forehead and said,

"Clan is a responsibility with no end,
Only a clansman can truly ken."

The one-and-a-half-finger girl said,

"I wish to see Padmalochan,
Maybe, somehow, I can restore his vision."

What was that low-caste, tiny little girl saying? However, seeing no alternative, the king called his son to the court.

The one-and-a-half-finger girl said,

"Prince, come to me by the door,
You must stand beside me; I can't reach far."

The prince was brought and made to stand next to the throne. The one-and-a-half-finger girl climbed onto the throne somehow and washed the prince's eyes with the spit of the frog's wife. She had kept the spit in a box tied up in a corner of her ghaghra.

The prince opened his eyes and saw the one-and-a-half-finger girl had restored his vision! He began to whine to his father that we would marry only her.

The king said, "Heavens! This is the daughter of a woodcutter! We don't even know her name!"

The girl said, "Nobody cared to name me. I am called the one-and-a-half-finger girl. I will name myself. My name is Pipilika Kumari."

The prince said, "Pipu, are you willing to marry me?"

The girl said, "I have three conditions."

"Go on," said the prince.

The girl announced, "My father is a woodcutter. The weaver gave me clothes, and the blacksmith forged my axe. I want representatives from all these communities—weavers, woodcutters, blacksmiths, potters, and farmers—at the royal court. The kingdom should take their advice, too. The old ministers should retire."

"And?" said the prince.

Pipilika Kumari said, "I have been wandering in the forest since birth. I will not be stopped."

"Alright, and?" said the prince.

The girl said, "The golden frog befriended me. His wife gave me the medicine to restore your vision. The grasshoppers, birds, and forest animals did not eat me; they spared my life. The forest is a space that gives shelter, and I want it, along with all its creatures, to be respected."

The king then gave the kingdom to the prince to rule. The prince accepted the three conditions and married the one-and-a-half-finger girl. Farmers, weavers, and blacksmiths rode to the wedding on grand chariots. They would become the king's courtiers after the wedding. The frog family came, too. The golden frog's father said, "My daughter-in-law's spit cured the king's son? What a girl! I welcome her into my family!"

There was light and only glory in the kingdom after this and forever!

SOMETHING TO THINK ABOUT

What is lineage? What is clan status? Are these things important? Is it right to insult someone because of their low birth or low caste?

THE STORY OF THE STORY

This was the story of a woodcutter's one-and-a-half fingers tall son. His small stature symbolized his low position in society. We have further developed the story. In one and a half fingers, the boy was replaced by a girl. Not only is our protagonist a girl but she is also tiny and low in social status. Her journey is thus even more difficult. More questions arise from her expedition.

Malanchamala

1

Like in the fairy tales, a wise sage arrived in the kingdom of the childless king and queen. He asked them to fast for three days and three nights and then travel to the Malancha orchard on the fourth day. They would find two perfectly yellowed mangoes hanging on the same stem. The queen should eat the fruit on the right, and the king should eat the one on the left.

After fasting as per the sage's instructions, the king took the queen with him after three days and went to the Malancha orchard. But plucking the fruit was a real bother. It wouldn't drop if they threw a stone at it; if they shot an arrow, the arrow bent. The tree couldn't be climbed. All the king's courtiers and men failed. In the end, one of the guards who lived in the village came and swiftly shimmied up the tree. The fruit fell. The king happily gave the guard one of his necklaces. Drums began to play, and even the elephants and horses started dancing.

During the meal, the king and the queen noticed that they had forgotten who would eat which side's fruit. The king said, "I am a king, I am a man. The fruit on the right is definitely for me." The king ate the fruit on the right, and the queen ate the fruit on the left.

In due time, a bouncing baby boy was born. Flutes and trumpets played. Drums played for ten days straight. Uncountable ponds were dug, and temples were established in the prince's name. He was named Chandramanik, the jeweled moon!

After the festivities, the queen noticed that the prince was getting thinner daily and wouldn't eat well. What was wrong with him?? The royal physician was called; he shook his head and said, "This boy's life is almost at its end."

A pall descended on the kingdom, where fireworks had been lit only moments before. The king and the queen were at a loss. On the twelfth day, the queen's maid, Malini, cried, "Help! I don't know what has happened! The prince has stopped moving!"

The queen fainted. The king was beside himself. The minister called the sage again. He was asked, "Is there any way to reverse what nature has decreed?"

The sage made some calculations and said, "If you see a beautiful girl, marry her to your twelve-day-old boy. Perhaps he will live if she is virtuous like *Sati*."

Who was Sati? In those days, people used to say,

"*She who washes clothes and plates,*
Cleans the home, never wakes late.
No matter what, her voice is never heard,
Be she pushed or slapped, never utters a word."

Where could they find a Sati, the same age as the newborn prince? A two- or four-day-old girl could hardly have the qualities of Sati. In those days, twelve was the right age for girls to get married. Thus, a twelve-year-old girl was searched for.

The king then sent ministers, sentries, courtiers, and footmen to fetch such a girl. No one even asked if the girl wanted to get married. The king did not want to know whether the girl's parents consented. His command was absolute. If they needed a girl, they needed a girl. The ministers, sentries, courtiers, and footmen would lose their heads if they couldn't find such a girl.

Out went the announcement, loud and clear. Kingsmen combed the land corner to corner, to no avail! Frustrated and tired, they found themselves under the same mango tree. Suddenly, across the lake, the guard's daughter descended to bathe. The anklets on her little feet chimed musically. The bangles on her wrists rhythmically clanged against her vase. The ministers, sentries, courtiers, and footmen saw a girl approximately twelve years old who had come to bathe. "Whose daughter is she?" "Why, that's the guard's daughter, I think." "What? How can the guard have such a beautiful daughter?" Her anklets sounded like the humming of a butterfly. The mustard flowers swayed in the breeze when she walked through the fields. Flowers seemed to bloom when she smiled. What was her name? She lived near a mango orchard, so she was called Malanchamala, the garland of the orchard.

Word was immediately sent to the guard's quarter. His wife was adamantly against the idea. Were they mad? How could her daughter marry a newborn baby? And a sick, dying child at that! As a mother, how could she just throw her daughter's life away?

The guard knew that if the king's will was that his baby son marry the guard's daughter, he could not refuse. He could not stop his tears. The girl said, "Mother, dress me up. If I don't get married, you will be beheaded. Father, ask my father-in-law if I can return to this house after I become the royal bride."

The guard sent news through a messenger, but even that drove the king mad. Such a young girl and so many questions!! He said, "I will decide whether I let her go home later. Ask her to come now."

The girl sent another message. "I'm the daughter of a mere guard. Will the king and queen sit down to eat with me? Will they even let me touch them?"

The king replied, "The girl is very disrespectful; tie her up, drag her, and bring her here."

The soldiers brought the girl wearing a bridal Banarasi *sari* with a rope around her waist to the palace.

A small boy lay asleep on his mother's lap, wetting his dhoti. Malanchamala married that boy in soiled clothes, crying, "Wah, wah!"

2

The injustice to the little girl caused the palace's roof to collapse, and a fire broke out. But did the evil king understand the reasons behind these disasters? He just thought that the girl was unlucky.

Malanchamala was about to enter the royal bedchamber with the little boy when the king said, "Why is the boy not crying?"

The queen said, "He is weak—sometimes he cries, sometimes he doesn't."

But why would the king listen to her? He had been against Malanchamala right from the beginning. He said, "The girl must be a witch. She's killed my boy. If you can, bring my son back to life. If you can't, then you won't be spared."

The girl was scared to death. With the baby in her arms, she left to look for a doctor on that stormy night. The minister went along with her. The queen also wanted to go. But the king said, "She will go alone. Arrest her parents. They will be released only if my son comes back to life."

Malanchamala arrived at the royal physician's house. He answered, "It is not my job to save the prince. Cross the forest and go to the city. You will find the grand physician there."

Malanchamala said, "Minister uncle, don't let the king kill my parents."

The minister said, "I have no other choice."

What else could Malanchamala do? She entered the forest's thick darkness with the boy in her arms. She was just a girl, and she had to carry the burden of the child. As time went on, the child wilted further in her arms. Foxes chased after them. Hyenas encircled them, intending to eat the child. Malanchamala's legs no longer moved, but there was great kindness in her heart. She thought, "He's just a baby; how can I leave him at the mercy of foxes and hyenas?"

Malanchamala waited. She had to save herself, as well as the child.

Who knows how long she walked? After crossing the territory of jackals and hyenas, Malancha met the king of the jungle, the Royal Bengal Tiger. "Wow! What do I see? Not one but two human treats with soft, young meat—it'll be great fun to eat!" the beast exclaimed.

Malanchamala hugged the child to her chest. "Such a tiny baby won't fill your stomach, Mister Tiger; you eat me instead."

"I'm a tigress! You can call me aunty. You seem to be a kind-hearted girl. Is this your little brother?"

Malanchamala couldn't help but burst into tears. The tigress was the first creature to speak to her kindly in a long time. She told her everything.

Aunty Tiger said, "Oh dear me. Where do I get milk for this baby? Can you feed him my milk, girl?"

Malanchamala fed the baby with the tigress's milk. The baby prince finally began to stir. The tigress's husband exited the cave and said, "Wait. Let me scare the village people and bring everything the child needs."

In the afternoon, he returned with a pillow stuffed with mustard seeds, a glass to drink milk, a shell spoon, a towel, a dhoti to wear, a blanket, and even a kohl applicator. "I see the baby is growing strong with my milk," the tigress said. "You better stay here until the prince grows up."

"What other choice do I have?" Malancha thought. Her mother and father were gone; she was now an orphan. Aunty Tigress and Uncle Tiger truly loved her and Chandramanik deeply. She decided to stay there. Malancha and Chandramanik both grew together in the forest.

3

Years passed, and Chandramanik was now six years old. Malanchamala was a young woman of eighteen. She touched the tigress and tiger's paws and said, "Aunty, Uncle, please give us your blessings; we must take our leave now."

The tiger and tigress growled and protested, but Malancha said, "Chandra is old enough to attend school. I never got the opportunity to study. Let him at least."

Uncle and Aunty couldn't stop them anymore. The tigress and tiger bid a tearful farewell, walking them to the forest's edge.

Beyond the forest was another country with a great capital city. On the way there, Malanchamala walked around holding Chandramanik's hand. Chandra said, "Sister Malancha, I am hungry and thirsty."

Malanch loved Chandra very much. She was protective of him, just like a big sister. But where would she find food in the forest? After walking some more, she came across an orchard. *Ah, just like my old house*, Malancha thought. *The same shade of the Madhabilata tree, the same butterflies flitting around—who stays here, I wonder?* "Does anyone live here?" She called out.

A lady came out. "Who are you?" She asked.

"I am Malancha. Can we rest for a little while in your garden? This is Chandra. Can you give him some water, please?"

The gardener gave them water and some sweets. Malancha told her she knew how to bloom large, beautiful flowers and weave garlands. "I am old," the gardener replied, "and I can't see well. Stay with me and weave garlands for me, and in exchange, I'll give you food and clothing."

Malancha said, "I can stay if I can send the boy to school."

They lived there ever since. In the morning, Malancha picked flowers and made all kinds of garlands. Chandra helped out. Then, the gardener went to the market to sell the garlands. Malancha took Chandra to school.

Kushal Pandit's school was very famous in the city. The king's seven sons and one daughter also went to study there. Chandramanik was admitted to the school, too. And Malanchamala? She sat in the yard outside and listened to the lessons being taught with rapt attention. Hungry for knowledge, she ate whatever she could get her hands on. Kushal Pandit noticed a young girl who was not a student but sat in front of the school, listening to the lessons. Years passed like this, and eventually, Malancha turned twenty-one.

One day, Pandit summoned Malancha and said, “Daughter, I see you listening to the lessons every day. Do you understand what you hear?”

Malancha said, “Is there any limit to understanding?”

“Do you understand what your brother studies?”

“He learns lessons meant for children, and I understand them. Now, I listen to the lessons that the king’s seven sons are learning. They are my age.”

Chandramanik was the same age as the princess, and Malancha was the same age as the seven princes. But the princes got mad, very angry. She was a woman and a gardener, too. How could her intelligence compare to theirs?

They planned to put her down. They told Kushal Pandit, “Let her also take the annual exams with us.”

“But she has not had any formal education,” he replied. “It wouldn’t be according to the rules.”

“I can try,” Malancha said.

The princes said, “If you succeed, you will be named Champion of Debate. And if you fail, you will be our slave.”

“What nonsense! What are these conditions?” Exclaimed Kushal Pandit.

But the princes were all masters of their whims and fancies. They appeared the next day with a golden pen filled with ink and gold paper. Malancha came with Chandra’s straw quill. The princes’ inkpot got overturned. Not much could be written by them. Yet, golden words seemed to come out of Malancha’s straw quill.

Kushal Pandit thought this girl was goddess Saraswati herself. He declared Malancha the Champion of Debate, shattering the princes’ egos.

From that day, Malancha occupied a permanent place in the school. Everyone knew that she was Chandra’s unfortunate, unmarried sister. Kushal thought he would propose marriage to her when the time was right. Chandra knew that Malancha was his sister, and their parents had died long ago. Only Malancha carried the burden of truth on her chest. She didn’t know how long she would have to keep the secret.

4

Meanwhile, there was another danger. When Chandramanik was twelve years old, he fell in love with Princess Kanchi. The princes already couldn’t stand Malancha. And now their sister was in love with her brother, the son of a gardener! It was a disgrace to their caste, clan, and family. They were all red with rage.

The rose garland that the princess's maid bought from the market that day was woven in Chandramanik's house. The princess secretly brought that garland to the classroom. She put it around her dear Chandra's neck behind everyone's eyes. While playing, they decided to marry each other when they grew up.

When this came to the ears of her brothers, they beat Chandramanik black and blue. They tore his school books and broke his slates. After destroying the classroom, they dragged Kanchi to the palace. They didn't even listen to their teacher's commands. They just kept saying, "You gardener's son! You wove a garland and then put it around our sister's neck! How dare you?"

They refused to listen to Kanchi's pleas.

The king sent his foot soldiers. Who was the young boy who dreamed of marrying a princess? The king's men shackled Chandra's hands and feet, and he was thrown into prison. Kanchi was kept inside the palace.

Malancha cried uncontrollably. Who would save Chandra? Who would reason with the king? Then she remembered that Chandra was the son of a king, too! His father could fight with the king. She wrote a letter to her father-in-law, the king.

"Your son is still alive. He is twelve years old. But he is a prisoner. Please have him released.

Yours, Malancha."

Then, there was a great war between the two kings. However, Chandra's father was a less powerful king than Kanchi's father, and he lost. He was imprisoned along with his army.

Malancha saw no other way. Perhaps her Aunty Tigress and Uncle Tiger could do something beyond human capabilities. She told Kushal Pandit and her gardener aunt the entire truth.

"*I am not single; to Chandra, I was wed,*
In our homeland, they wanted me dead.
I raised him like a mother or sister, dear,
To protect him, I will not pause or have any fear."

The three of them then went to the forest.

5

Aunty Tigress and Uncle Tiger were their last hope. "My dear, you're back after so long!" Aunty said. "Where did that baby I breastfed go?"

Malancha said, "Aunty, the king has put him in jail for the crime of being friends with the princess. Everyone in his father's kingdom is imprisoned too."

The tigress's eyes lit up. She said,

"*Growl, roar, growl,*
I'll go to town.
Those who made Chandra cry,
I'll bring them all down!"

That night, tigers attacked the massive palace of the great king—not one or two, but an army of a hundred tigers. They ate the sentries, the vizier, the courtiers, and everyone else. They broke open the jail and freed Chandramanik and his father. They told the princes and the king, "Apologize quickly. Otherwise, we will end your entire bloodline."

The older king trembled and apologized to the younger king. A peace treaty was signed—it was decided that the two should be classmates; then, when they reached marriageable age, if Chandramanik and Kanchi still liked each other, they would be married.

The younger king was hesitant. How could he say that his twelve-day-old son was married to a twelve-year-old girl? How could he say that they would be forever grateful to her? She was the girl who saved Chandra! Her consent had not been taken during Chandra's first marriage. Would her permission not be taken even during his second marriage?

Finally, the king expressed himself in front of everyone. Then Malanchamala came forward and said, "I didn't give my consent during that marriage, so I don't consider it a marriage at all."

Rumors buzzed in the meeting. Malancha said, "Life is not a game and foolish beliefs shouldn't let you turn other people's lives into games. Eating fruit does not make a baby. And that baby will not survive illness just because he gets married."

Kushal Pandit said, "Of course! Some stupid things like this are also written in the ancient texts, but we don't believe those."

Malancha said, "I have raised Chandra. Like a child, like a mother. He calls me 'sister' but treats me like a mother. I love him. He is not my husband. But he means a lot to me."

The king said, "Can I ever thank you enough?"

Malancha said, "I might get married. I might not. It's not a big deal. I want to spend the rest of my life in our gardener Aunty's orchard. And I want to study many texts with Kushal Pandit."

Her mother-in-law, the queen, had also arrived. She said, "But, my dear, when Kanchi becomes the king consort, you will become the queen mother. The people will worship a virtuous girl like you. And your parents? They are also alive; they have been in jail since then. Now, they can stay with us in the palace if they wish."

Malancha said,

"To be worshipped, I don't want
My virtues I do not flaunt.

I have walked along for days on end,
I have forgotten the meaning of friend.

Now, why keep me in the cage?
Tell my parents I am well,
My wisdom has saved me from many a hell."

Chandra came and hugged Malancha. He said, "Don't leave me. I can't live without you."

It was then decided that Chandra, who was still a child, would study in Kushal Pandit's school, along with Kanchi. Malanchamala would also study there. Sometimes, Chandra's parents would come to visit him; Malanchmala's parents would also visit sometimes.

Forgetting the differences between the rich and the poor, the high and the low, and men and women, they began building another world in Kushal Pandit's classroom. The gardener Aunty fills the classroom with the smell of flowers day and night.

Will you go to their classroom one day?

SOMETHING TO THINK ABOUT

Twelve days or twelve years—are any of these suitable ages for marriage? Why did Malanchamala say, "To be worshipped, I don't want."?

THE STORY OF THE STORY

Thakurdar Jhuli's story 'Malanchamala' *is popular in Bengal, especially in West Bengal. Another variant of the story is* 'Rupoban Kanya'. *In that story, a teenage girl named Rupoban is also given in marriage to the infant prince.*

Be it "Malanchamala" or "Rupoban," those girls in the story are tolerant. They almost risk their lives to prove they are as virtuous as Sati. In those stories, the king is much crueler; he cuts the girl's nose and ears. In that story, the boy has no healthy relationship with the girl. The girl serves him from afar through Malini Masi, the gardener. Finally, Chandramanik marries Kanchi. The father-in-law realizes his mistake and shelters Malanchamala in a corner of the house, which makes her happy. Kanchi becomes the queen consort. Malanchamala becomes the queen mother.

Is this how someone's life is meaningful? Can such child's play be considered marriage? Our new story thus creates a new Malanchamala.

The End or The Beginning?

The golden boy's night turns to noon through story and rhyme,
Our golden girl, in her faraway dreams, has a lovely time.
Sleep, child; rest your head in the golden dust of that land,
Fruits, sweets, milk, and treats will lie in wait and stand.
A new day dawns, a new flower blooms when you wake,
Weave new tales with new words with every step you take.

Satabdi Das

A Kolkata-based story-teller. Is professionally entrusted to help in the learning of pupils, but is more akin to aid in their unlearning. A Disrupter. Unsettles things for six days a week and recreates them on day seven. The same has been done here, with renowned Bengali folklore. This is how fairy tales read when retold by the granddaughters of ancient witches.

Nadia Imam

A translator bringing her first translated work to life with a wish for happily-ever-afters all around! She is based in Kolkata and has an English literature degree. Nadia aspires to change the world, one word at a time. She dreams of closing cultural divides through translation so that every tale she touches has a chance to connect, uplift, and leave readers a little more hopeful.

Paramita Brahmachari

A student of first literature, and then film from Jadavpur University, Paramita Brahmachari comes pre-addicted to all good books and visuals. Despite having a doctorate in Film Studies, and no training at all in graphics, she has been making covers since 2016, mostly as an excuse for reading yet more books, and imagining how stories unfurl in lines and colours.
She has won the Oxford Bookstore and the Publishing Next awards for cover design, but this is her first time ever illustrating for children.